# Herefordshire Folklore

# Herefordshire Folklore

*by*
**Roy Palmer**

**Logaston Press**

LOGASTON PRESS
Little Logaston Woonton Almeley
Herefordshire HR3 6QH


First published by Logaston Press 2002
Copyright © Roy Palmer 2002

ISBN 1 873827 58 X


Set in Times by Logaston Press
and printed in Great Britain by
Bell & Bain Ltd., Glasgow

*Dedicated to the memory of Dave Jones (1940-91)*
*singer, musician, dancer, impresario*

# Contents

# Acknowledgements

I am indebted to Heather Hurley, who turned up the tale of Tom Reece's ghost and other Hoarwithy stories, and also passed on information from her researches into the pubs of South Herefordshire; to K. Stanley Yapp, who supplied much material on Leysters; to Thony Handy, who as well as dancing with Leominster Morris is its meticulous archivist; and to my wife, Pat, who transcribed music, took photographs, and accompanied me on many pleasurable explorations of Herefordshire.

I should also like to thank Herbert Baber, Joyce Banbury, John Buchanan-Brown, Alan Buckwell, Mairi Calcraft-Rennie, Daphne Davies, Peter Garnett, Mary Hirons, G.F. Halley, Bob Jenkins, Annie Jones, the late Lavender Jones, the late Rob King, Stuart Knight, Tony Malpas, Maureen Martin, Douglas Miller, Brian Nixon, Mary Parker, Roger Pye, the late Miss S.F.G. Robinson and the late E.P. Thompson. I am also grateful to these institutions: Bodleian Library, Folklore Society, Hereford Cathedral Library, Hereford Record Office, Herefordshire Libraries, *Punch* Library and Archive, Royal College of Music Library, Trinity College (Cambridge) Library, Vaughan Williams Memorial Library (London).

For illustrations I gratefully acknowledge Corpus Christi College, Oxford & Bridgeman Art Library p.7; Mary F. Collins p.138; Ben Corbett pp.36, 102, 108, 109, 119; Daphne Davies p.170; Betty King p.143; Valerie Grosvenor Myer pp.31, 62; Hereford Cider Museum p.136; Hereford Museum and Art Gallery pp.111, 112, 206 (top); Hereford Library pp.4, 141, 207 (Alfred Watkins items) & p.208 (other items); Mrs. Jean Hopkinson and Mrs. Anne Orgee p.75 (top); John Howes p.201; Annie Jones pp.177, 183, 189, 191; Leominster Morris pp.185, 188, 215; Leominster Priory Church p.80; Logaston Press pp.5, 9, 11 (top), 99, 162; Mr. and Mrs. Masefield p.43; Much Marcle Church p.84; Pat Palmer pp.6, 15, 19, 22, 23, 26, 40, 42, 44, 52, 56, 57 (top), 59, 60, 86, 92, 121, 123, 124, 125, 126, 127, 130, 147, 211, 214; Mrs. E. Priday 142; Michael Raven p.140; Reed Midland Newspapers p.67; Gill Richards p.76; Mrs. B.M. Rhys (for Marjorie Wight items) pp.14, 64, 65, 137, 200, 209, 216; Catherine Side p.205; Malcolm Thurlby pp.53, 55; Mrs. Ursula Vaughan Williams pp.170, 176, 197. Music set by Gordon Ashman pp.140, 165, 197; and Robert Kay pp.171, 176, 177, 191.

# Introduction

Herefordshire's amalgamation with Worcestershire for local government purposes in 1974 proved predictably unpopular. Old loyalties led to persistent campaigning, especially on the Herefordshire side, and after 23 years, in 1997, the two counties' separate status was restored.

In my book, *The Folklore of Hereford and Worcester*, published by Logaston Press in 1992, I commented on the state of 'unholy wedlock' which existed, and looked forward to the expected divorce. It now seems logical to separate the accounts of the two counties' folklore, and I have started with Herefordshire. The original material has been not only extracted but revised and supplemented. Illustrations and music examples have been considerably increased.

I should have liked the title of *The Folklore of Herefordshire*, but that belongs to the seminal study by Mrs. E.M. Leather which first appeared in 1912 and has been re-issued more than once since. My adoption of *Herefordshire Folklore* will, I hope, avoid any confusion.

At the beginning of the 21st century in Herefordshire certain customs of the past—celebrating at wells, greeting the dawn on May Day, wassailing apple trees in winter—have been revived, and attract an enthusiastic following. In addition new patterns are emerging, driven apparently by communal impulsion rather than conscious desire to innovate. The creation and tending of roadside shrines where deaths have occurred, the placarding of birthdays and other anniversaries on improvised billboards at the approaches to towns and villages, the introduction of fireworks to mark the New Year: all these are new phenomena or the reappearance of old. They seem to show that something more than technology is needed if people are to feel at home in their lives and in their environment.

Interest in folklore and its changing manifestations seems likely to continue well into the 21st century—and no doubt, beyond.

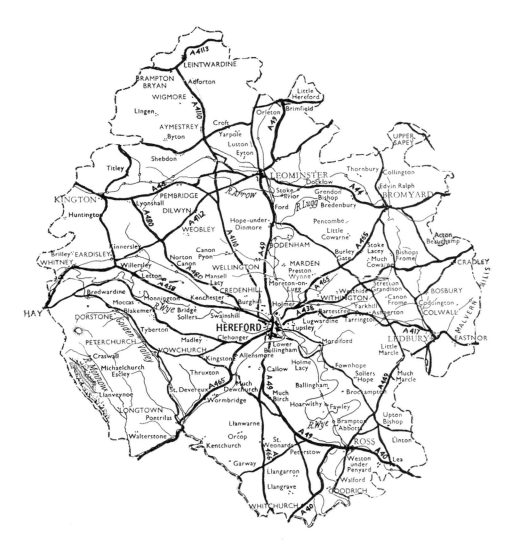

*Map of Herefordshire dating from 1938*

# CHAPTER 1

# Places

Hills and caves, wells, springs and streams, rocks and stones, fields and farms, even single trees: all these have been or are the subject of beliefs, traditions and stories. Towns and villages have popular etymologies and long-standing reputations, not always of the best. But one of the functions of folklore seems to be to provide possible explanations—unscientific but not unsatisfying—of how people's everyday surroundings came about.

### Pride and prejudice
Sayings like 'All about Malvern Hill a man may live as long as he will' certainly express local pride. Herefordshire boasted its six W's—wool, water, wood, wheat, wine (cider) and women—but shared with several other counties the disparaging rhyme:

> Herefordshire born, Herefordshire bred,
> Strong in the arm, weak in the head.

Even so, natives are proud to be known as 'white-faced uns', after the county's breed of cattle.

The mention of several places—including Letton, Orcop and Pencombe—once elicited the invariable comment of 'God help us', a reference to the fabled poverty of their inhabitants. People of Orcop had alternative responses such as 'Lord be praised' (in summer), 'where the sun never sets' or 'where the treacle mines are'. Pencombe was also said to be where they:

> Put the pig on the wall to watch the band go by,
> And thatched the river to keep the ducks dry.

Its neighbour suffered the taunt of:

> Little Cowarne, wooden steeple,
> The cracked bells, wicked people.

Luston, labelled (or libelled) as 'the dirtiest place you ever did see', was characterised as:

> Luston short and Luston long,
> At every house a tump of dung.

At Weobley 'they sweep the tide away with a broom', the reference being to a stream liable to cause sudden floods. Other expressions are more obscure. Were people advised to 'go to Ross and be sharpened' because the town represented quickness of wit? Why was Ballingham Hill a spot 'where the sun never shines'? Why did Ledbury people say that God dumped at Woolhope all the rubbish left over after the world was made? The same village appeared in a poor light in this rhyme:

> Lusty Tarrington, lively Stoke [Edith],
> Beggars at Weston [Beggard], thieves at Woolhope.

The first line was varied to 'Dirty Tarrington, lousy Stoke', presumably when spoken by those from outside these villages.

A given place could attract both disparagement and praise. Those travelling to Bosbury from Malvern were advised to make their will beforehand. People in the village boasted that it was bigger than Hereford until a Saxon warlord

*Bosbury in 1881*

*Vowchurch*

came along and announced: 'If I can take big Bosbury, I can take little Hereford'. He took and destroyed Bosbury, which never recovered; but he failed to take Hereford, which prospered.

Fanciful, perhaps, but no more so than the tongue-in-cheek suggestion that the names of Vowchurch and Turnastone came about because a do-gooding but quarrelsome woman said to her sister: 'I vow I will build my church before you turn a stone of yours'. There may well have been rivalry between the builders of the two churches which face each other across the River Dore, but the names respectively mean multi-coloured church and thorn thicket.

## Stones
Before the days of precise maps, rivers and stream made very good boundary markers; in their absence, so did great stones. At Colwall the (relatively small) stone near the Crown Inn, which formerly stood closer to the centre of the crossroads, was once called Arthur's Quoit. Some stories suggest that it was indeed thrown when two unnamed giants quarrelled over territory, and agreed that one should hurl a stone from the Malvern Hills and that both should accept where it fell as their boundary. Alfred Watkins heard a different explanation: a jealous giant living in a cave on the malverns 'saw his wife with another fellow down at Colwall, and chucked a big stone at her, which killed her'. (Some say that he wrenched the stone out of the hillside, this creating Clutter's Cave. This

in turn is said to have provided a hiding place for Owain Glyndŵr and Sir John Oldcastle). However, a roadman whom Watkins met in the Yew Tree Inn at Colwall Green told him that 'the devil was carrying it in his apron, the string broke, and there it fell'. A further contention is that when it hears midnight strike the stone turns round nine times. The operative word here is 'when'. In fact the stone has been in its present position only since the late eighteenth century when it was dragged there from a quarry at the foot of the Wyche by a team of oxen. Why anyone went to this trouble remains unclear.

The Whetstone on Hergest Ridge above Kington is reputed to go down to the Buck Brook to drink when it hears the morning cock crow. It may be a waymark but its name, a corruption of 'wheat stone', possibly derives from a time of plague in the fourteenth century when supplies of corn and other produce were left there for Kington people to collect.

In a field just off the road, three miles out of Hereford on the way to Sutton St. Nicholas stands the Wergin Stone, one of two which marked a boundary or pointed a safe route across the water meadows when the River Lugg flooded them. A cup-like recess may have been used to deposit an annual payment of some kind. In 1642, according to a contemporary account, the stones were driven a considerable distance across the flooded meadow by 'a mighty wind'. At the time, 'a man of Mr. James Seaborne's, which was riding to Hereford, did see one of the Stones going, and as he relates, a blacke Dog going before the Stone'. Afterwards, nine pairs of oxen were needed to pull the bigger of the stones back to its former position. Daniel Defoe, who picked up the story when he visited Herefordshire in the 1720s, says the stones moved 'about twelve score paces'. Late in the nineteenth century, both stones were still in place, but only one now remains, somewhat disfigured by metal guardrails.

*The Wergin Stone as photographed by*
*Alfred Watkins in the early 1900s*

*Arthur's Stone, above Dorstone*

Arthur's Stone, the most famous in Herefordshire, took its name from the local belief that Arthur in a desperate fight with another king, broke his back and buried him there. The site—in fact an uncovered chambered tomb—is on Merbach Hill between Bredwardine and Dorstone. Parson Kilvert, who spent the last years of his life at the former place, knew Arthur's Stone well. Joseph Gwynne told him in 1878 that one of the stones had imprinted 'the marks of a man's knees and fingers' to be seen were 'made by King Arthur when he heaved this stone up on his back and set it upon the pillars'. Some who still feel that the site has a mystical aura, and conduct ceremonies there. In 1992 a brass chalice and bowls in which incense had been burned were discovered. Police commented that such finds were not unusual. Various offerings are left, and pentangles and signs of the zodiac painted on adjacent turf.

In his classic book, *The Old Straight Track* (1925), Alfred Watkins included a chapter on stones which were among the indicators of ley lines. Watkins (1855-1935), brewer, archaeologist and pioneer photographer, first propounded in 1921 his theory of alignments which he called ley lines. Ancient trackways, trading routes and burial paths established these lines, which were marked by various features of the landscape and also standing stones. His work attracted both support and ridicule. Half a century after his death a secondary cult of ley lines emerged, which claimed that they were conduits of energy through the earth. Some connected them with UFO activity. Others thought the entire concept fallacious. In a damning verdict on the original theory, L.V. Grinsell wrote: 'My own impression is that the prehistoric Britain of Alfred Watkins ... had no existence in the form in which he presented it except in his own imagination and that of his followers'. Nevertheless, articles and studies continue to appear on Watkins, and his own book remains in print.

## Hills

Malvern Chase, consisting of some 6,000 acres in Worcestershire, 600 in Herefordshire and a mere 100 in Gloucestershire, was given by Edward I to Gilbert de Clare, the Red Earl of Gloucester. Clare assumed this to include parts of the parishes of Colwall and Eastnor, but these belonged to the diocese of Hereford. Bishop Cantilupe (for whom, see also chapter 2) complained to the king, who in January 1278 referred the dispute to two local justices, Rauf de Hengham and Walter de Helyn, and a jury drawn equally from Herefordshire and Worcestershire. When justices and jurors visited the contentious site the earl attended in person, as did the bishop—in full canonicals.

*The Red Earl's Dyke*

The finding, announced in April 1279, favoured Cantilupe; Clare was ordered to construct a ditch to delineate the boundary. He is a said to have begun digging in person, and to have set a pattern of throwing up the spoil on the Hereford side, so making it easier for deer to jump into his territory than out of it. The ditch, known as the Red Earl's Dyke, was probably not completed until 1287, five years after Cantilupe's death, It is still visible, over 600 years on, and it constitutes a stretch of boundary between Herefordshire and Worcestershire, Herefordshire and Gloucestershire.

One of the peaks in the Malvern chain, the Herefordshire Beacon, otherwise known as the British Camp, s reputed to have been the place where in 50 A.D. Caractacus (now normally called Caratacus), prince of the Atrebates, made his last stand against the Romans. Some disagree. Fosbroke, the historian of *Ariconium*, says that Caractacus was indeed at the British Camp, but retreated across Herefordshire to a cluster of strong positions—the *montes ardui* (steep hills) mentioned by Tacitus—near the confluence of the rivers Clun and Teme: Borough Hill, Tongley Hill, the Whettleton Hills and Coxall Knoll. He argues

1704 the elder branch of the Nanfan family was extinguished, and the malediction transferred to a junior branch which itself died in poverty at Worcester in the nineteenth century.

The Raggedstone is very firmly in Worcestershire, but the 'accursed shadow', according to Rev. H.L. Somers-Cocks, was 'firmly believed by old residents of Eastnor and of other parishes near'. At the same time, Somers-Cocks reported an alternative explanation for the curse: that it was uttered by Druids making a last stand against Roman attackers on the hill who, as they were about to die, called down a malediction on those on whom its shadow should fall.

Hills much less majestic than the Malverns, and even homely

*Previous inn sign at the Tump Inn, Wormelow, commemorating Arthur*

tumps, have their stories. Wormelow is a hamlet a few miles south of Hereford on the Monmouth road. Nennius, the ninth-century antiquarian who may originated in Ergyng (now the part of Herefordshire known as Archenfield), wrote that the tump at Wormelow was the place of burial of Anir, the son of King Arthur. The mound itself, he reported, 'sometimes measures in length seven feet, sometimes fifteen feet, and sometimes nine feet'. The belief persisted locally that no one could twice step over or round the tump with the same number of paces. There is still a Tump Inn and a Tump Lane, but no tump, since this was removed in the nineteenth century during a road-widening scheme.

Further south on the same road, the A466, lies the hill-top village of St. Weonards (locally pronounced St. Wonnards). People believed the obscure Welsh saint (for whom, see also chapter 3) to be buried beneath the mound near the church in a golden coffin on top of a golden chest inscribed:

> Where this stood is another twice as good,
> But where that is, no man knows.

In 1855 archaeologists, inspired, perhaps by the story, excavated the mound, unfortunately removing in the process a tree which served as the village maypole. They discovered two cremation burials, but no golden objects. Folk memory proved to have at least some basis, as is often the case. The feasts and morris dancing which took place on the tump would not be possible today, since it is densely wooded. Revellers who once lingered there too late—until the church clock chimed midnight—ran the risk of meeting a phantom pig at the nearby crossroads.

Just south of the village, a standing stone shares a story with many other places in England. One night, a sheepstealer is carrying home his prize on his shoulders, its legs tied together in front of him. He stops to rest with his back to the stone, and hoists his burden on to it. The dead sheep slips down behind, pulls the rope against the man's neck, and strangles him. Next morning he is found dead, a convenient warning to others.

Cobbler's Mound, just to the east of Shobdon, near Leominster, takes its name from the tradesman who encountered the devil close by. Asked whether Shobdon was thereabouts, the cobbler—members of whose trade were renowned for independence and even radicalism—quick-wittedly replied: 'No. I'm looking for the same place myself'. Then, indicating the bag full of shoes for repair which he was carrying, he added: 'I've worn out all these while I've been looking'. Thwarted in his plan to obliterate the fine church at Shobdon, the devil threw down the huge shovelful of earth he was carrying for the purpose, and so created the mound.

A coda to the story adds that when the villagers heard of the encounter they were afraid that the devil would try again, and therefore dismantled the church. In fact, the twelfth-century building was indeed taken down and rebuilt in 1756 on the orders of the landowner, Richard Bateman, who had the Norman chancel arch, two doorways and their tympana re-erected as a landscape feature on his estate, Shobdon Park. Local tradition holds that Lord Bateman acted because the bells in the original church shook up his wine.

A variation on the theme of hill creation crops up a few miles away, close to Kings and Canon Pyon. Two conical hills marked on the map as Pyon Hill and Butthouse Knapp, near the A4110, are locally called Robin Hood's Butts. One tradition is that the devil created them by emptying sacks of earth there after being dissuaded from overwhelming Hereford with them. Either he swallowed the suggestion that Hereford was so wicked as to be on his side already, or he accepted a trusty cobbler's familiar tale of wearing out a large number of shoes on his way from the city.

A different story claims that two giants attempted for a wager to jump over Wormsley Hill to Canon Pyon. Each clipped the top, knocking out enough earth to form one of the smaller hills. In a further tale the devil is replaced by Robin Hood and Little John, each carrying a spadeful of earth to bury the monks at Wormsley but abandoning it to form one of the hills. In the 1880s, as a boy in Ledbury, John Masefield was told yet another story:

*Pyon Hill and Butthouse Knapp, near Canon Pyon*

Robin Hood used to stand on one [hill], to shoot at the other; then crossed over ...., picked up the arrows and shot them back. ... Another man ... said that they were Robin Hood's treasure rooms, and that there was an underground passage between them.

## Below Ground

Real finds such as the one at Burstners Cross must have stimulated the many traditions of buried treasure. Bronsil Castle—now a ruin, near Eastnor—still keeps the secret of the whereabouts of a hoard of gold and silver concealed by Lord Beauchamp before going on crusade. Beauchamp told his wife that if he died the treasure would be easily found, provided his body was brought home for Christian burial. When he was killed outside Jerusalem his remains were

*The Buck brothers' view of Bronsil Castle in 1731*

11

indeed brought back to Bronsil, though the treasure could not be recovered. The practice was for the flesh to be boiled off a corpse, and the bones only to be returned. If some of these were lost in transit, perhaps the condition laid down by Beauchamp remained unfilled. It seems that the croak of a raven, perhaps a descendant of the tame bird Beauchamp set to watch over his hoard, can be heard at midnight close to the place where the treasure still lies.

A variation on the story claims that a resident spirit at Bronsil frequently kept the household awake at nights until the then owners, the Reades—this was either late in the reign of Elizabeth I or early in that of James I—went to Oxford to consult a wise man. Following his advice, they sent to Italy for the first Lord Beauchamp's bones, and in due course buried them. Peace ensued at Bronsil, but when the Reades (still in occupation) fled during the Civil War when the castle was burned, for some reason they dug up the bones and took them to Lugwardine. This is what caused the raven's protests.

Another bird, this time a jackdaw, stood guardian over the treasure hidden at Penyard Castle, near Ross-on-Wye. There, two hogsheads full of money were in a vault protected by iron doors. A farmer dragged the doors open with a team of twenty steers, revealing barrels and sentinel jackdaw. Overjoyed at the prospect of reaching the treasure, he called out: 'I believe I shall have it'. Immediately the doors clanged shut and a sepulchral voice intoned:

> Had it not been for your quicken-tree goad and your yew-tree pin,
> You and your cattle had all been drawn in.

According to Alfred Watkins, a 'crock of French gold' came to light at Castle Farm, Madley, early in the nineteenth century. So said the granddaughter of a servantmaid present when the find was made in the cellar. The same farm also has a ghost, and a reputed passage leading to the church a mile away. Kinnersley Castle, a mansion of the the late sixteenth and early seventeenth century, is said to have a similar tunnel running to the nearby church. The priory of St. Guthlac at Hereford was likewise linked to its vineyard on the banks of the Wye. This passage was investigated by Watkins, who found it to be 'some kind of natural "fault" or long crevice, not man made'. It seems that religious establishments on either side of the Wye at Foy, four miles from Ross, were indeed linked by a subway beneath the river. This began in what is now the rickyard at Court Farm at Hole in the Wall, and reached the cellars of Ingestone House on the Foy side. 'A native questioned about 40 years ago', wrote A.H. Lamont in 1920, 'said he ventured in, when a young man, to about the middle of the tunnel, accompanied by his dog. Either his courage failed or some obstruction prevented his further research'. Ingestone (pronounced 'Inkstone') House is where James I was allegedly entertained by aged morris dancers (see chapter 9).

Stories of such passages could be capped with accounts of whole settlements swallowed beneath the ground. A field by Arthur's Stone is said to have, deep below it, a village engulfed by an earthquake. People claimed to be able to see the top of the old church steeple at the bottom of a pond in the field.

The Wonder, still marked on Ordnance Survey maps, is the site of a great landslip on the eastern side of the ridge above Much Marcle, which lasted for several days. A chapel at Kynaston was destroyed, together with a number of farm animals. People were understandably alarmed, and some thought the end of the world was nigh. The Wiltshire antiquary, John Aubrey (1626-97), a frequent visitor to Herefordshire, wrote:

> The Wonder, in the parish of Much-Marcle, is the place, where some acres of ground with trees growing on it, did in Queen Elizabeth's time move. 'Tis true, 'tis a desk-like descent, but sliding here could be none, because of the great asperities there left and the rocks.
>
> So 'tis pleasant to behold the cracks (now overgrown with Ivy) and the caverns, which is a good hint for other rocks, cracks, and mountains. A boy first discover'd this motion, and brought home the news, that the Sheep-cote did walke; they open'd the dore of the sheep-cote, and let out all the sheep before it fell. This motion overturn'd the Chappel; the bell of which now hangs in Sir John Kirles gate-house [at Homme House] in the parish. This asperity of ground is about 2 or 3 acres.

A much greater disaster, if the tale is to be believed, was the loss of Old Pembridge in Shobdon Marshes. A fiddler who had played for a dance at Pembridge arrived home at Eardisland, then remembered a fine pair of white gloves tied with red ribbons which he had left behind. He retraced his steps, only to discover that the village had disappeared into a swamp. Until the twentieth century people believed that a stone dropped down a well on the site could be heard striking the top of the church spire far below.

## Wells and Waters

Herefordshire was particularly famed for its large number of healing and holy wells. There were three at Peterchurch alone, two for eyes and one for rheumatism. The stories of others—at Dorstone, Hereford, Marden and Stoke Edith—are told in chapter 3. Some now seem to be only a name on a map—Harold's Well above Much Marcle, for example—their history lost. Jacob's Well at Bosbury, once renowned for curing eye troubles and boils, now seems to be unknown to villagers. Bromyard's Eye Well still exists, in a private garden in Highwell Lane. The water of St. Waum's Well on the Malvern Hills, just below Waum's (or Clutter's) Cave, was often drunk by John Masefield who knew of its power 'to cure broken hearts, weary eyes and rheumatism'. By the 1950s, though, he found the spring dry—not surprisingly, because the water had been diverted as a supply to Eastnor.

Until within living memory St. Anne's Well at Aconbury was prized for its healing powers. (Anne, the reputed mother of the Virgin Mary, is frequently associated with wells). Speaking in 1990, a local forester, Arthur Crum, recalled seeing as many as twenty or thirty people at times washing their hands and swilling their faces in the water. They were 'mostly city folk from Hereford', he said, somewhat wryly. At midnight on Twelfth Night (5 January) a blue mist was reputed to rise from the well. Water drawn then—known as 'the cream of

*The Pot Well, Craswall*

the well'—was carefully bottled and saved to be used when its curative powers were needed. The well is still there (on private land), cut into solid rock at the back of a thirty-yard recess, but tangled undergrowth points to its present neglect.

Craswall owes its name, first recorded in 1231 as Cressewell, to the well which still exists below the churchyard gate. Even so, its Holy Well is more famous: sometimes called Pot Well because of its semi-spherical stone trough, lies outside the village near the ruined priory.

According to a local tradition at Brinsop, St. George, who is depicted on the tympanum over the church door, killed the dragon in a nearby field at what came to be called the Dragon's Well. A humdrum manhole cover now marks the mythical spot.

Higgins Well at Little Birch acquired its name in the manner described in a letter to the *Hereford Times* by H.W. Southey in April 1900:

> The story runs that originally the waters ... had their outlet at the top of this meadow [off the road leading from Aconbury Hill to Little Birch Church]. The occupier, who was also the owner, became so annoyed by the trespasses of the villagers across his land to the well that he had it filled up, and, as he supposed, effectually closed. Shortly afterwards,

however, whilst smoking his pipe in the great chimney corner of his house, he was startled by a sudden eruption of water under his feet. The spring had forced a new outlet at a spot which seemed to indicate to his untutored mind that there was a guardian spirit of some sort in existence quite equal to the emergency of protecting popular rights. The farmer was determined, however, that the spring should not be re-opened on his land. So he went to the foot of the meadow, and on the road side dug into the soil until the water bubbled through the underlying rock. With the opening of the new adit the inrush in the chimney corner disappeared. The genii of the spring had been appeased by the honorable amends made by the irate farmer, and the latter through his act of contrition acquired a local immortality by having his name for ever afterwards associated with the well.

To commemorate Queen Victoria's jubilee in 1897 villagers raised money to restore the well's surrounding walls and basins. A similar sense of local pride emerged just over a century later at Luston, where the overgrown holy well as a millennium project was cleared out and the surrounding area re-paved. On Midsummer Day in 2001 the Lustonians dressed their well with a wide variety of flowers, and listened to hymns sung by the Leominster Harmony choir. They plan to make the ceremony an annual event.

Rivers and streams have their own traditions. The Wye has an extensive literature of its own, including verses written in 1848 to the tune of *The Sea* by Thomas Vaughan, Hereford tailor, poet and ballad singer:

*Well at Luston*

The Wye, the Wye, the faithful Wye,
Is pleasant to the stranger's eye:
I love on its sun-lit stream to gaze, -
Or nightly pace its darkest maze,
She sports within her banks so green
And. playful glides from scene to scene;
I never was on the wild, wild sea,
But I love to ride on the gentle Wye,
Where bounding billows doth not come
To whelm me in a wat'ry tomb:
Wo gloomy waste, nor murky sky,
Doth mar thy beauties, lovely Wye.

Against this one should set the traditional belief that the Wye is a greedy river, requiring an annual victim. After a child had been drowned near Bredwardine a woman is said to have reassured mothers about the safety of their children with these words 'You needn't worry about them, m'dears. The river has took his toll and they'm safe for the rest of the year'. Bodies of the drowned were thought to rise on the ninth day. The number may not have scientific backing, but it is certainly of mystical significance.

When a bell was allowed to fall into the River Lugg at Marden, a water nymph made sure that it stayed firmly at the bottom. A wise man said the bell might be recovered if a team of white freemartins (heifers) were to pull it with yokes of yew tied with bands of wittern (rowan), provided the whole operation were carried out in complete silence. As the bell broke surface the nymph was seen in it, asleep. As it started to come up the bank one of the drivers, unable to contain his excitement, said:

In spite of all the devils in hell,
Now we'll land Marden's great bell.

The mermaid—or rather rivermaid—awoke, and plunged back into the river with the bell, breaking the yokes and screaming:

If it had not been
For your wittern bands
And your yew tree pin
I'd have had the twelve freemartins in.

The story is very similar to that of the buried treasure at Penyard Castle (see p.12). A bronze hand bell which can now be seen in Hereford Museum was found eighteen feet below ground level in a pond a few yards from Marden Church in a field belonging to the vicar. The question arises as to whether the find inspired the story or confirmed it.

Henry Tudor's experience was happier than that of the Marden villagers. As he crossed the River Arrow between Pembridge and Eardisland. He took the opportunity to remind his followers of the ancient saying that 'he who would win a national strife must shoot the arrow first'. Kington angling club until at least the mid-1950s had a 'no wading' rule when fishing for trout in the Arrow, which was siad to date back to the time of Henry Tudor.

The Sapey Brook near Clifton-on-Teme was renowned for a series of circular marks on its sandstone bed. Two—at Jumper's Hole (for which, see also chapter 7)—were particularly clear, with other good specimens between Clifton and Stanford Bishop. Most scholars agreed that the marks were caused simply by the action of the water, though one argued that prehistoric beasts had made them. Tradition says that St. Catherine of Ledbury (see also chapter 3) and her servant, Mabel, lost a mare and colt to a thief one night as they were travelling this way. To avoid leaving tracks the robber led the animals along the brook, but St. Catherine prayed that the prints should remain visible. By this method the animals were traced to Ledbury, and recovered. The thief turned out to be a girl wearing pattens. The telltale signs were to be seen for centuries in the brook.

## What's in a name?

Placenames are deeply embedded in our history and. culture. Some are simple and homely, remaining evocative when preserved in the streets which have covered fields such as Goose Acre, Broad Meadow, glebe or leasow (grass-land), croft or pleck (small field). Others may appear outlandish but are readily explained. For example, the Asps at Richards Castle is land with aspen trees; the Clappers at Hentland, a field with rabbit burrows; Oyster Hill near Colwall, the place of a sheepfold; Pirricroft at Donnington, a peartree orchard; the Quab at Brilley, a bog; Yays Meadow at Marden, land beside a stream. One has to admit that still others have become totally incomprehensible: the Cloggat (Ewyas Harold), the Gliss (Winforton), the Grout (Aylton), Tink-a-Tank (Marden), Twinkler (Ledbury), the Weet (Richards Castle), and many more.

History, real or imagined, lies behind certain names. Apostles Farm at Kingswood is so called because St. John himself is supposed to have preached there. The nearby Apostles Lane and Apostles Stone are logical extensions; incongruously, where the latter crossed the Kington-Hereford road a gibbet once stood. Dead Woman's Thorn, recorded at Eastnor as early as 1580 and still shown on Pathfinder maps, may mark the place of a demise or killing, though the details are irrevocably lost. On the other hand, Deadwoman, near the former Vine Tree Inn at Ross, may have been a wry name for a boundary marker. Even so, stories circulated that the stone commemorated a woman torn to pieces by hounds, or alternatively, murdered while fetching water from a well. Kildane Meadow, Field and Orchard at Bromsash are claimed to commemorate the killing of Danes ordered by King Ethelred on St. Brice's Day (13 November) 1002.

Another slaughter occurred at Scotland Bank, just north of Dorstone, under Bach Hill. The local vicar, George Powell, told H.J. Massingham:

> The tradition is that after the Battle of Worcester [1651] the remnant of the wild Highlanders found a refuge there but were surrounded by the Welsh. Wary of coming to close quarters with these stalwarts and their claymores, the Welsh set their dogs on them and they were torn to pieces to a man.

Massingham comments that: 'this may well be a true story handed down from the impression of its horror for centuries'. It would indeed be chilling, though one wonders what the Scotsmen were doing so far west; and the word Scotland, meaning land subject to tax (or scot), was often applied to boundary fields—one example is at Burghill. (There is also a Scotch Graves field name at Weobley).

A Welsh presence in what is now south-west Herefordshire was achieved at a stroke of the pen in the 1550s when a great tract of land, to the west of Offa's Dyke transferred from Wales to England under the terms of Henry VIII's Act of Union. The Welsh *llan* still appears in seven village names: Llancillo, Llancloudy, Llandinabo, Llangarron, Llanrothal and Llanwarne. Several other places have alternative Welsh names: Garway (Lann Guoruoe), Kenderchurch (Lanncinitir), Kentchurch (Lan Cein), Kilpeck (Lann Degui Cilpedic), Much Dewchurch (Lann Dewi Ros Cerion) and Sellack (Lann Suluc). Forms of Welsh, sometimes mixed with English, occur in large numbers of field and farm names, such as *cae*, field; *tref*, small settlements and later, single farm; *cyfar* (anglicised to cover), land worked

*The Eardisley Oak*

jointly. All these are widespread south-west of the Wye; the last occurs on thirty-six farms in Ewyas Lacy alone. *Cae*, pronounced 'ca', 'car' or simply 'c', is particularly common in Clodock and Rowlestone. Examples include Cae Pwll (pool field), Cae Quarry, Cae yr Inn, Cae Gnoll, Cae Derry (oak tree field), Cae Groes (crossroads field), Cae Gwyn (white field), Cay yr Pistil (spout/spring field), Car y Ffynnon (spring field), Cay yr Jack Crouch, Gay y Graban (corn marigold field).

*St. Augustine as depicted in stained glass in Huntington Church*

Further Welsh names crop up, sometimes disguised, in considerable variety. Moneyfarthing Hill at Clodock comes from Mynydd Ferddyn—Ferddyn's Hill. The Mynde, also from *mynydd*, is found at Ballingham and in other parishes. The Saison at Kenderchurch means Englishmen's farm; and at Rowlestone Pulch y Hoont presumably signifies mole's gap. Even well away from the south-west corner of the county one encounters Kymin (rock field, from *cae maen*) between Westhide and Ocle Pychard, the curious Court y Park near Trumpet, and no doubt others.

Inevitably, the collective memory of field names has been eroded by population movement, housing development and agricultural change which has amalgamated small fields into large units. Fortunately, the Woolhope Society's survey of over 125,000 field names in Herefordshire has produced a map for every parish, so a published record is available to supplement oral tradition,

There are many Gospel Oaks and Holy Thorns in Herefordshire (see chapters 3 and 10). The Eardisley Oak, half a mile from the village, remains a venerable landmark. Stanford Bishop claims (among other places) to have been the site of the oak under which St. Augustine of Canterbury met British bishops in 603. The tree is long gone, but the saint's chair is preserved in the church—although dendrochronology in fact dates it to the early medieval period. The

Three Sisters, as they are called, are yew trees standing on Rushock Hill near Kington, close to Offa's Dyke. They were planted in the eighteenth century to mark the memory of three sisters who lived at Knill Court, though some say they commemorate three shepherds lost in a bitter snowstorm as they tended their flocks.

# CHAPTER 2

# People

Saints, sinners, soldiers and a prize-fighter provide a varied portrait gallery of figures who have left their mark on the folklore of Herefordshire. To this day, Hereford Cathedral is jointly dedicated to St. Mary the Virgin and Ethelbert the King, the latter of whom met his death at Sutton Walls before being canonised. Thomas Cantilupe, a thirteenth-century bishop of Hereford was also to become a saint. By contrast, both Owain Glyndŵr and the probably-mythical Jack of Kent were believed to possess occult powers. As in many counties, the Civil War left persistent traditions in Herefordshire, with Bosbury, Brampton Bryan, Goodrich, Hereford and Ledbury featuring prominently. Finally, Tom Spring, prize-fighting champion of England in the early nineteenth century, is still remembered in his native Fownhope.

## Saints

By the River Lugg at Marden the church of St. Mary stands close to where the body and severed head of Ethelbert, king of East Anglia, were thrown into a marsh on the orders of Offa, king of Mercia, in 794. The first surviving account of the story, *Passio Ethelberti* (the suffering of Ethelbert), is in Latin, and dates from the early twelfth century.

Ethelbert, aged fourteen, succeeds his father as king and is persuaded to seek a bride. He sets off to meet Aelfrytha, the daughter of Offa, and his queen, Kyndrytha. As he mounts his horse the earth shakes, terrifying his escort. During the journey the sun suddenly becomes obscured and the skies only clear when Ethelbert prays. He reaches the royal villa at Sutton (or possibly Marden), and there:

> While he slept, he saw the roof of his palace collapse, its walls fall away from vaulted chambers, and his mother, the queen, coming to him, beating her breast and rightly shedding genuine tears, the clothes she wore, soaked in blood. He saw a great wooden beam, long and wide,

raised up on high in the middle of the royal city, from the eastern side of which he saw blood dripping from a fracture and from the south, a flashing column of light reaching up to heaven. He himself was changed into a bird, whose golden wings covered the beam, and in swift flight it flew upwards from whence he heard a sweet symphony from the highest throne of the Trinity.

Ethelbert arrives at court, greatly impressing Aelfrytha by his demeanour. Offa, however, has heard rumours that Ethelbert has designs on his land, and, egged on by Kyndrytha, calls for a volunteer to kill him. Winbert, who has a grudge dating back to Ethelbert's father's time, agrees. He asks for Ethelbert's sword before ushering him into Offa's presence and uses it immediately after they enter the chamber to decapitate him. On the orders of Offa the corpse and head are thrown into a marsh by the Lugg. A column of light 'flashing in splendour' immediately arises at the spot.

Three days later Ethelbert appears in a dream to a man who with a companion takes up the body and head, washes them in river water, and puts them on an ox cart to take them to Hereford. On the way, at Lyde, the head falls off. A blind man stumbles against it, and his sight is immediately restored. The remains are finally buried, and the faithful gather at the place, seeking a cure 'from all disagreeable diseases'.

Unsurprisingly, the story was often varied or embroidered. According to one suggestion, Offa's wrath arose because Ethelbert attempted to seduce Kyndrytha. Alternatively, she tried to seduce him, and when he rejected her advances informed Offa that Ethelbert had approached her. A variant

*Marden Church*

held that Kyndrytha, jealous of her daughter's admiration for Ethelbert, told Offa that he should be killed because the match would make him too powerful.

Another account suggests that the queen drugged Ethelbert's wine before he was murdered; yet another that she draped over a pit a cloth on which Ethelbert sat and fell to his death. Old maps showed part of Sutton Walls as the King's Cellar, which was traditionally taken to be the pit in question. On the other hand, a different tradition placed Offa's palace on the site of the present vicarage at Marden.

Scandalised by the murders Aelfrytha took a vow of chastity and went to live as a hermit in the marshes of Crowland in Lincolnshire at a place which later became St. Guthlac's Abbey. Offa became fearful of retribution and arranged to give a tenth of his goods to the church. He also went on a pilgrimage to Rome, where Pope Adrian directed him to build a church of wattle at the site of the first grave and a church of stone (later to be the cathedral) at Hereford.

The spring which gushed forth from the first site at Marden was incorporated in the church, where St. Ethelbert's Well can still be seen (though not by the casual visitor, since the building is now kept locked). A second St. Ethelbert's Well, where the ox cart paused on its journey, was near Castle Green in Hereford. The transport of Ethelbert's body to Hereford was in fact ordered by Eadwulf, bishop of Lichfield, and it is possible that it was carried down the Lugg and up the Wye. A coffined or shroud-wrapped corpse could well have been put down temporarily at the top of Quay Street after being landed. The tomb of St. Ethelbert in Hereford Cathedral where the sick were healed and the feeble-minded restored to reason was destroyed in 1050 by marauding Danes. Ethelbert is not forgotten in East Anglia, where he is the patron of eleven churches. His

*Site of St. Ethelbert's Well,*
*Castle Green, Hereford*

23

influence made Hereford second only to Canterbury as a centre for pilgrimage in mediaeval England.

John Philips put his own gloss on the story in the poem, *Cyder* (1708):

> And *Sutton*-Acres, drench'd with Regal Blood
> Of *Ethelbert*, when to th'unhallowed Feast
> Of *Mercian Offa* he invited came,
> To treat of Spousals: Long connubial Joys
> He promis'd to himself, allur'd by Fair
> *Elfrida's* Beauty; but deluded dy'd
> In height of Hopes — Oh! hardest Fate, to fall
> By shew of friendship, and pretended Love!

Thomas Cantilupe or Cantelupe (1218-82) would have been well aware of the cult of St. Ethelbert. His uncle, Walter, was bishop of Worcester. His studies included both law and theology. He was ordained as a priest in 1245, lectured in Paris, served twice as chancellor of the university of Oxford, and for a short time as chancellor of England. In 1275 the canons of Hereford Cathedral elected him as bishop.

He was red-haired, short-tempered, learned, austere—a hair shirt wearer, and no doubt charismatic. One day as he was travelling from his palace at Stretton Sugwas towards Hereford the cathedral bells rang out of their own accord to welcome him. The White Cross erected at the spot where he heard the bells has been restored or renewed over the years.

Cantilupe became embroiled in a dispute with the archbishop of Canterbury, John Pecham, and was excommunicated by him. He travelled to Italy to appeal to the papal court, but died before matters could be resolved. Part of his body was buried at Orvieto but his heart and bones were brought

*St. Thomas à Becket (left) and St. Thomas Cantilupe in stained glass at Credenhill*

back to Hereford by his secretary and friend, Richard Swinfield, who succeeded him as bishop.

During the journey miracles occurred. At Hereford the bones began to bleed in the presence of the Red Earl who had quarrelled with Cantilupe over boundaries between their land (see chapter 1). The tomb attracted so many visitors that in April 1287 Swinfield made the decision to move it from the Lady Chapel to a more prominent position in the north transept. The occasion was important enough for King Edward I to attend in person. Masons were nonplussed as to how to move the heavy structure. Two young pages found they could lift it without effort, but afterwards no one could then move the tomb from its new position. A cripple who touched it was immediately restored to health.

Within a month, 71 miracles were reported. The tally 20 years later reached 221 (by some accounts 400), and the pope sent a commission to Hereford to investigate. The cases included not only those already mentioned but people cured of paralysis and brought back to life after hanging or drowning. Some claims were found to be fraudulent; others stretched credulity to breaking point. In four weeks the commission investigated seventeen cases and on the strength of these recommended that Thomas be canonised. In 1320 he officially became St. Thomas of Hereford, the only saint ever to have died excommunicate.

Through his cult, added to that of Ethelbert, the cathedral drew large numbers of pilgrims whose gifts helped to pay for the great west tower. As late as 1610 some of St. Thomas's relics were secretly carried through the city by night in time of plague, 'giving total succour to the same'. Yet some thirty years later, early in the Civil War, the bones were all dispersed.

## Sinners

In Kentchurch Court hangs the portrait of a man with ascetic, careworn face whom some say is St. Jerome (because of the emblematic lion in the background and the cardinal's hat that is just visible at the back of the figure's neck). Others suggest either Owain Glyndŵr or Siôn Kent, rector of Kentchurch in Glyndŵr's time. Both have been credited with other-worldly powers.

Strange portents accompanied Glyndŵr's birth according to Shakespeare, who also makes him say (in *Henry IV*, Part I), 'I can call spirits from the vasty deep. ... Why, I can teach you, cousins, to command the devil'. Even contemporaries had similar thoughts when English armies attempting to put down Glyndŵr's rebellion in Wales repeatedly seemed to have to face atrocious and unseasonable weather. Despite winning many battles, Glyndŵr ultimately lost the war, but having disappeared in 1412 was never betrayed or captured. His death went unrecorded and his place of burial remained unknown.

Strong and persistent traditions linked Glyndŵr's last, hidden years with Herefordshire, where lived three of his daughters, married to Englishmen: Janet at Croft Castle, Margaret at Monnington-on-Wye, Alice at Kentchurch Court. There are tales that Glyndŵr visited Croft disguised as a shepherd; that he was buried in Monnington churchyard beneath a flat, broken stone by the porch; and that he lived in secret at Kentchurch Court. Members of the family into which Alice married still live there, and in 1999 John Scudamore decided to reveal a secret passed down by word of mouth for almost 600 years. Owain Glyndŵr, he said, was buried not at Monnington-on-Wye but at Monnington Court, near Vowchurch, behind the present farm buildings. Geo-physical surveys showed structures beneath the mound, including a possible chapel, and an excavation discovered bones, which were sent for carbon dating. Unfortunately, the test results do not seem to have been made public.

Glyndŵr at one stage is said to have adopted the pseudonym of Siôn Gwent, and it is possible that in so doing he contributed to the genesis of a mythical figure called John or Jack Kent. Both are associated with Kentchurch Court, where in addition to Glyndŵr's tower, Jack Kent's stable (a cellar) and his bedroom (where on stormy nights a ghostly shape issued from the panelling) were once pointed out.

Various other candidates have been proposed as prototypes for Jack, or contributors to a composite character. John Kemp, archbishop of Canterbury in 1452, seems rather a far-fetched suggestion. More plausible are Dr. John Gwent, a Chepstow-born Franciscan friar with a reputation for miracle-working who died in 1348; and the fifteenth-century Dr. John Kent of Caerleon, astrologer and author of a book on witchcraft. The Siôn Cent already mentioned seems to have sympathised with the reforming Lollards, and he alludes to the rebellious Sir John Oldcastle in one of his poems.

*Monnow Bridge near Grosmont*

Whatever their origin, stories about Jack of Kent probably circulated orally long before the middle of 1589, when Anthony Munday wrote his play, *John a Kent and John a Cumber* (printed 1595). They certainly continued to be told long afterwards within a particular area including parts of Herefordshire, Monmouthshire and Gloucestershire.

John, Jack or Jacky makes a pact with the devil in which he receives supernatural powers in exchange for his soul after death, whether his body is buried inside or outside a church. However, he does not hesitate to trick the devil. Their jockeying for mastery is illustrated by several stories about the bridge over the River Monnow on the road from Kentchurch to Grosmont. Jack undertakes to build the bridge (in one night, say some versions) with the help of the devil, who agrees to bring stones for the purpose from Garway Hill. The devil can only work in darkness, and when cock-crow signals dawn he has to jettison an apronful of stones, thus creating (according to the variant followed) rocks on Garway Common, the Seven Sisters at Symonds Yat or the Devil's Lappit above Tintern. In return for his work the devil claims the soul of the first to cross the finished bridge but Jack outwits him: he rolls a loaf of bread over and a little dog chases it; he is thus the first across, but animals have no souls, so the devil is thwarted. A different twist is that Jack agrees to cross first, and does so, but argues that his shadow has preceded him in the moonlight, so the devil must be content with that. Jack stays shadowless for the rest of his days.

Once Jack goes from Kentchurch to London with a mincepie for the king. He sets off at daybreak and the pie is still hot when he arrives in time for breakfast. On the way he loses a garter which is caught in a church weathercock as he flies past. Back at home, a farmer wanting to go to Hereford Fair tells Jack to keep the crows out of the corn while he is away. Later in the day he comes across Jack at the fair and furiously asks him what the game is. Jack assures him that the crows are not in the corn, and when the farmer returns he finds the crows sitting in an old barn with no roof. A big bird is keeping order, perched on an old beam, and the farmer takes this to be the devil.

One Christmas Jack is preparing to drag a Yule log into a house when some bystanders remark that it was too heavy to be taken inside. In response he fetches four goslings and harnesses them to the log, which they then draw to the hearth with ease.

One day the devil challenges Jack to thresh a whole bay of corn in a single day. Jack takes off his boot and puts it on the stack, where it kicks down the sheaves one by one. He sets a flail on the floor and it threshes corn by itself as he sits playing the fiddle and murmuring from time to time:

> Nobble, stick, nobble.
> Play, fiddle, play.

The task is finished well within the allotted time.

On another occasion, Jack offers the devil his choice of the pigs in a consignment. When the devil picks those with straight tails Jack feeds them beans so that their tails curl. Next time the devil chooses curly tails so Jack drives the animals through water to make their tails go limp. In a field where the wheat is just springing up Jack asks the devil whether he prefers tops or butts. He chooses butts, so when the harvest comes he has the straw, and Jack the corn. The following year the devil changes to tops but since the field has been set with turnip seed Jack has the better bargain once more. In a grass-mowing contest he wins again by sticking harrow tines into the devil's ground so that his scythe constantly loses its edge.

Some of these trials of wit or strength left marks on the landscape, or so we are led to believe. One of the explanations of Robin Hood's Butts (see also chapter 1) is that they were produced by spadefuls of earth thrown from Burton Hill by Jack and the devil. An alternative source for the rocks on Garway Hill is that the devil dropped them when he was helping Jack build a fishpond at Orcop, and could not pick them up because a crowing cock announced the coming of day.

The time came when Jack's death approached, and his score with the devil would have to be settled. To circumvent the agreement about burial inside or outside a church, Jack chose to have himself interred within the thickness of the church wall at Kentchurch (or Grosmont, or Skenfrith, say other versions), thus being neither in nor out. In the Grosmont version we are told that Jack gave deathbed instructions that his 'liver and lights' were to be exposed on spikes projecting from the church tower. He predicted that a dove and a raven would come to fight over the remains, with a victory by the former showing that his soul was saved. The outcome remains in doubt.

## Soldiers

The English Civil Wars of the seventeenth century, probably because they involved internecine strife, left a deeper impression on the popular imagination than many later conflicts. Oliver Cromwell, who remained a bogeyman for generations was said to have won the decisive battle of Worcester on 3 September 1651 thanks to bartering his soul to the devil in exchange for victory. When he died, seven years to the day afterwards, the violent storms which swept across the country were taken to show that the devil was taking his own. At Brampton Bryan, where the tempest proved particularly strong, the devil was thought to be dragging Cromwell across the parkland, knocking down trees in his path.

The reason for the supposition was that the Harleys of Brampton Bryan Castle were for the Parliament. In 1643 during the absence in London of her husband, Sir Robert, Lady Brilliana took over command and resisted attacks

*The old gateway to Brampton Bryan Castle*

led by various Royalist commanders, Fitzwilliam Coningsby, Sir William Vavasour and Sir Henry Lingen. Only when Charles I was obliged to raise the siege of Gloucester in September 1643 did Brampton's attackers give up after seven weeks, and march away, leaving the village destroyed and the church demolished. The Webbs in their monumental history of the Civil War in Herefordshire, describe Lady Brilliana as 'a woman of rare resolution, fit to command, and to ensure obedience'. Her own voice can still be heard in letters she wrote to her oldest son, Edward, a parliamentary officer: 'My comfort is that you are not with me, least they should take you; but I do most dearly mis you. I wisch, if it pleased God, that I weare with your father'. Shortly after the siege, Lady Brilliana, 'overworn by fatigue and excitements sickened and died'. The following spring the castle again came under Royalist attack, and fell after prolonged resistance.

*Lady Brilliana Harley*

*Goodrich Castle before the undergrowth was cleared*

By late 1645, though, the whole of Herefordshire was under Parliamentary control, save for Goodrich Castle. The attacking force there was commanded by Colonel John Birch, whose effigy (he died in 1691) can still be seen in Weobley Church. Birch's niece, Alice, had fallen in love with Charles Clifford, a member of the Royalist garrison and contrived to join him in the castle. In attempting to run away together they plunged one dark night on horseback into the turbulent waters of the Wye, and were both drowned. In stormy weather, or so runs the tale, they can be seen struggling in the water, their desperate cries muffled by wind and wave.

The garrison, under Sir Henry Lingen, held out until July 1646, when supplies were exhausted and the walls were beginning to crumble under the pounding of cannon fire they had sustained. The Royalists were allowed to surrender. They marched honourably out to the strains of a lively tune called *Sir Harry Lingen's Fancy*. The music does not seem to have survived, even though, according to the Webbs, it was 'long used in the neighbourhood in the dances of the peasantry'. A copy is rumoured to exist somewhere in the 200 boxes of the Foley Estate papers held in Herefordshire Record Office. (Thomas Foley of Stourbridge bought the Lingen lands when the family had to sell them to pay fines levied by Parliament after the Civil War).

Other towns and villages have tales, oft-told and long-remembered, of the war. In April 1645 a Parliamentary force led by Colonel Massey in Ledbury came under surprise attack at dawn by Royalists under Prince Rupert who had marched overnight from Leominster. A fierce running battle developed in the High Street and the Southend, and also in gardens and alleys behind, together with the churchyard, as the Parliament men withdrew towards their base at

Gloucester. As a child John Masefield was told that 'Prince Rupert charged down Church Lane at the head of his men', which might have been difficult, considering its narrowness. Nevertheless, the stonework above the church's north porch still shows the marks of musket balls. Other slugs dug out of the west door are on show in St. Katherine's Chapel, together with a sword found hidden long after the battle. A further skirmish of some months later is commemorated by a plaque on the Talbot Hotel in New Street.

A few miles away to the north, at Bosbury, this inscription is still legible on the churchyard cross: 'Honour not the + but honour God for Christ'. It is said to have been inscribed on the orders of the then vicar as part of a bargain struck with Parliamentary soldiers who wanted to pull the cross down as a symbol of popery. Even so, they destroyed most of the stained glass in the Morton Chapel, and also the stoup for holy water in the south porch. As they marched off, one soldier turned and fired a shot through the east window, which explains why one small pane there is of plain glass. The series of incidents features in a lively historical novel, *In Spite of All* (1901), by Ada Edna Bayley (writing as Emily Lyall), who visited Bosbury, where her brother was the parson.

Lyall also wrote of the Hopton family, Parliamentary sympathisers whose house at Canon Frome was plundered by Royalists in 1642. Several years later when the place was again in Parliamentary hands, and under attack by Royalists, the King's Carpenter, John Abel, constructed a 'sow' or siege engine, 'a tower of wood, mounted on wheels, and drawn by oxen, with rooms loopholed and musket proof one above the other, enough to overlook all the works, and with a door and bridge for entrance'. The device seems to have been abandoned when Royalists, led by Sir Barnabas Scudamore, marched off towards Malvern on receiving news that a big Parliamentary force was approaching from Corse Lawn in Gloucestershire by way of Ledbury.

*Church Lane, Ledbury*

31

*Old Cross at Bosbury, with Emily Lyall's grave,*
*marked by a smaller cross, to the left*

Thomas Swift, vicar of Goodrich and Bridstow for thirty-four years, died in 1658 at the age of 62. He had ten daughters and three or four sons, one of whom was the father in due course of Jonathan Swift, the writer of *Gulliver's Travels*. Thomas Swift, fiercely devoted to the Royalist cause, went to Raglan Castle in 1645 to offer the king his coat. When the governor, Sir Charles Somerset, remarked that it was of little worth, Swift rejoined 'then, take my waistcoat'. Paradoxically, this proved to have 300 gold pieces sewn in, a sum which Swift had raised by mortgaging some of his land.

There is also a story, reported by the Webbs, that Swift, 'having a head mechanically turned, contrived certain pieces of iron' with four spikes which he threw into the Wye when he knew that the 'rebels' were to pass that way, and caused them to lose 'two hundred of their men who were drowned or trode to death by the falling of their horses, or torn by the spikes'. It is inconceivable that Swift invented the caltrop, which is the name for the device described, since it was recorded as early as 1519, but he could well have had some made, possibly by the village blacksmith. Certainly, caltrops have been found in the Wye near Goodrich. Charles I undoubtedly visited Raglan Castle in 1645, and there is a tradition that in the same year he slept at least once in 'the old Chamber on the E. side of Church Lane' in Hereford. Until some time in the nineteenth century boys from the Cathedral School processed to the house on 29 May, each with a 'slip of oak', and sang in the flower-decked street. Plum cakes and ale were distributed to all who attended the ceremony.

## Prizefighter

Just off the road between Fownhope and Woolhope stands a monument erected in 1954 to Tom Spring, prizefighting champion of England in the early 1820s. He was born in the hamlet of Rudge End in 1795, the son of a butcher called Winter. Spring, one of those nicknames which go by opposites, he eventually adopted as his own.

Young Thomas intended to be a butcher like his father, but chance determined otherwise. By the age of 18 he was already famed for his athletic prowess, and when his dancing partner at a village wake was insulted by 'the bully and terror of the neighbourhood, a big and mature miller', Tom lashed out. He then won the fight which inevitably followed.

Tom Cribb, a former champion boxer, may have heard of this. When he was visiting Hereford he sought out Tom Spring and persuaded him to seek his fortune as a bare-knuckle fighter. The often-lengthy contests attracted huge crowds, who bet heavily on the outcome. Rounds ended only when one man was knocked down, and a fight ended only when a contestant failed to come up to scratch (a line drawn on the ground).

Tom Spring had twelve fights, of which he lost only one. At the Pitchcroft (now the racecourse) at Worcester, in front of 40,000 spectators, he fought the Irish ex-seaman and mercenary soldier, Jack Langan, over two hours and twenty minutes. His victory did not please the six Irishmen who turned up at Spring's public house in Hereford, the Booth Hall, and offered to give him a good thrashing. Spring coolly went upstairs to change into fighting rig, then took on all six and threw them out after administering a severe beating.

On the other hand, printers of street ballads rushed out blow by blow accounts, cast into rough verse, such as *Spring and Langan. A New Song*, published as far away as Gateshead:

> Ye champions all both far and near,
> I pray now give attention,
> For Spring he is the finest man,
> Of any we can mention;
> A champion came from Ireland,
> And Langan was his name, sir,
> Who thought to beat our champion Spring,
> And bear away the fame, sir.

> *Chorus*
> For Englishmen will not be bet
> By any other nation,
> For is they will fight man to man
> They're sure of a good thrashing.

JACKSON.

Molineux, (the Black.)

SPRING.

Richmond, (the Black.)

Sutton, (the Black.)

But oh let's hope that ne'er a one,
From any other nation,
Will e'er be fit to take the belt,
From the English nation.
January was the appointed time,
And the 7th was the day, sir,
That these two champions did meet,
For to decide the fray, sir.

A stage was then erected for
Those champions so bold, sir,
It's for to fight with all their might,
For the belt which Spring now holds, sir;
But all the cry it was that Spring
Was sure to win the day, sir,
For Langan he will ne'er be fit
To take the belt away, sir.

At twelve o'clock or something more,
They mounted on the stage, sir,
They both were stripp'd, each fac'd his man,
And eager to engage, sir.
The Irish champion said to Spring,
I've come to let you know, sir,
The belt I'll strip from your shoulders.
Whether you will or no, sir.

You'll find your mistake, then says bold Spring,
And that I'll let you know sir,
I'll send you back to Ireland,
Full of grief and woe, sir;
Hats off, they cried around the stage,
When they begun the fight, sir,
And Langan swore that he would kill
Our champion Spring outright, sir.

The first 9 rounds that they did fight,
Langan was sorely beat, sir,
Then the friends of Spring did loudly sing,
20 to 1 we'll bet, sir;
That Spring the champion of our land
Their favourite will defeat, sir,
And send him back to Ireland
His sorrow to relate, sir.

Then Spring with cunning begun the fight
For to get on more bets, sir,
But for 20 rounds or more
He appeared to be quite weak, sir;
The friends of Spring were up to that,
The odds they still kept betting,
And Langan's friends took up the same,
Till they found that Spring was skeeming.

CRIB.

For they began to smell a rat,
And found out Spring's intention
To lead them all into a stake,
And leave their pockets empty;
But as for Langan we must say,
He is just as good game, sir,
As ever came from Ireland,
Or any other place, sir.

2 hours and more it's they did fight,
There stood unto their station,
With courage both these heroes fought,
For the honour of each nation.
Now Langan says I'll fight no more
With your champion Spring, sir,
For the beating I have got from him
I'll remember while I live, sir.

LANGAN.

45 rounds these heroes fought,
With courage on the stage, sir,
A better fight has not been seen,
Not for this many an age, sir;
Hard blows on both sides were received,
No bribery was taken.
Langan said to Spring, I'll give in,
For you've thrash'd well my bacon.

MENDOZA.

So we'll drink and sing in praise of Spring,
In all his undertakings,
And that he ne'er the belt may lose,
But always thrash their bacon;
Says Spring to Langan you are bet,
After your great boasting,
You know you swore that you would be
The champion of this nation.

RANDALL.

I say neither Irish, Scotch, nor French,
Nor any other nation
Shall e'er be champion of this land,
While Englishmen are reigning;
So boast no more o'er Englishmen,
Spring unto Langan said, sir,
For Englishmen before they're bet
Will die upon the stage, sir.

You boxers all now drink a health
To Spring upon the stage, sir,
And if any other man comes forth

*Tom Spring's memorial at Rudge End, Fownhope*

# THE LIFE AND DEATH OF
# THOMAS WINTER SPRING.

We once had a Champion, his name
  was Winter Spring.
A man both upright and kind,
By high and low esteemed he was loyal
  to his Queen,
So brave and so noble was his mind.

Chorus.

Then lay down the belt so low, the
  gloves on his tomb stone throw,
Thomas winter spring, was an honour
  to the ring.
And he's travelled to the shades below.

He boldly fought and beat Jack Langan
  Ward and Neate,
And all who opposed him in the ring,
There never was a man, who was born
  on Britain's land,
Could speak disrespectful of Spring.

He was born as you shall hear in fam-
  ed Herefordshire,
Where all did the champion adore,
They presents him did give, and they
  wished him long to live,
But alas poor Spring is no more:

He did oppression hate, no advantage
  would he take,
He was allways manly and right,

But boldly in the ring we could depend
  on Spring,
For honour and glory he would fight.

Poor Tom Spring was never bought, all
  his battles well he fought,
In is praise Old England would sing,
All classes far and near, so delightfully
  would cheer,
And their motto was Victory & Spring

We have left you all do know, Tipton
  caunt and Bendigo,
And numbers connected with the ring,
But search all o'er the land, you will
  never find a man,
To equal poor Thomas winter Spring

Britons will record his praise, while in
  the tomb he lays.
And call him an honour to the ring,
A marble stone complete, shall be pla-
  ced at head and feet,
Saying here lies poor Thomas winter
  Spring

In Holborn he did dwell and he was
  respected well,
And when his neighbours looked upon
  his bier,
There did many grieve full sore, saying
  alas he is no more,
And for Spring was shed many a tear.

But tom was doomed to go, and lay in
  the shades below,
And his leaving caused the ring, to de-
  plore,
And honest britons say, in his grave be
  happy lays,
Alas ! Thomas Spring is no more.

Then lay down the belt so low, the
  gloves on his tombstone throw,
Thomas winter Spring, was an honour
  to the ring,
And he's travell'd to the shades below.

T. Hodges Printer, Toy and Marble Warehouse, 31, Dudley Street, Seven Dials.

*Ballad,* The Life and Death of Thomas Winter Spring

He soon will be engaged, sir;
To lose the fame of England
We then should think it hard, sir,
But while we have such men as Spring
We defy the world at large, sir.

Of course, Spring fought other opponents, but his encounters with Langan seem to have aroused the greatest interest. Their return match at Birdham Bridge, some three miles from Chichester, took place in January 1828. Spring won once more, and his victory again inspired ballads such as *A New Song on the Great Fight between Spring and Langan*, printed at Bristol, which concludes with these verses:

These heroes fought on & the battle it rag'd
Like fam'd Waterloo so hotly engaged;
One thousand bright sovereigns, that was the stake,
If I win, thought Paddy, a man of me 'twill make.

Seventy-eight well-fought rounds they boldly contended,
Full an hour & 3 quarters before it was ended,
When Spring he tipt Paddy a blow so rum,
And time being called to the scratch he could not come.
Old England still the belt has in store,
The brave Irishman has been beaten once more.
Paddy Langan & 'tatoes are now both outdone
And brave Spring in cyder toasts every one.

By this time Spring had left the Booth Hall in Hereford to take over the Castle Tavern in London's Holborn, and shortly after the second Langan fight he retired from the ring. He died in 1851, and was buried in West Norwood Cemetery. In *Boxers and their Battles* (1900) Thormanby wrote: 'There is no name on the long roll of British boxers more worthy of honour and respect than that of Tom Spring. He was one of Nature's gentlemen—brave, honest, courteous, big-hearted—a true friend and a generous foe'. The ballad writers made their own valediction (see previous page).

# CHAPTER 3

# Churches

Sited in 'God's Acre', the church was once spiritually as well as physically the focal point of most villages and towns. Its central place in the climactic moments of birth, marriage and death is examined in the next chapter. Here are accounts of builders and bells; epitaphs and inscriptions; stories in wood, stone and stained glass.

The first memorial inscriptions in this country were in the time of the Romans. The earliest tombs in parish churches date from the twelfth century but tombstones in churchyards came into common use only from the seventeenth century onwards. Even then, the poor seldom enjoyed the luxury of epitaphs. Inscriptions are now carefully controlled but in earlier times a wide range of styles from pious to punning was tolerated. As one might expect, saints bulk large, but there are also a few sinners—and scandals. Finally, the churches have their own traditions, some decayed but others still vigorous.

**Builders**

Church sites were often chosen—or so persistent reports would have us believe—by supernatural means. At Leominster a holy man of the seventh century dreamed that a lion fed from his hand. The same night Merewald, king of Mercia (who happened to be nicknamed 'the lion'), dreamed that a hermit had news for him. Next day the two chanced to meet and when the hermit related his dream the king gave orders that a church should be built at the spot. The figure of a lion is still to be seen by the great west door. Despite this belief the name of the town is thought by many to derive from 'Leofric's Minster'. Leofric, earl of Mercia, who died in 1057, is best known as the husband of Lady Godiva. A less prosaic derivation is that the the town's name has Welsh origins in Llanlliene—'the church in the district of the streams'.

The original church at Clodock in the far south-west of Herefordshire was built in the sixth century. An account written some 600 years later tells how the site was chosen. A young noblewoman fell in love with Clodock (or Clydawg),

*St. Edith's Well, Stoke Edith*

king of Ewyas (and grandson of Brychan, the saint-king of Brecknock), and swore to marry no one else. Another man who had designs on the lady took advantage of a hunting trip with Clodock to murder him. When the body was found it was loaded on a cart to be taken to Ewyas Harold but the oxen stopped on the bank of the River Monnow and refused to go any further. There Clodock was buried. A column of fire played over the grave and a spring burst from the ground. A decision was taken to erect a church at the place, but builders preferred another site at Llanwonog, over a mile away. A start was made there but masonry laid each day collapsed at night until the builders returned to the bank of the Monnow. Nothing now remains of their work—the earliest parts of the present church of St. Clodock date from the twelfth century—but the story is not forgotten. St. Clodock's Well is on the river bank not far from the church.

Another saint's well still runs with limpid water at Stoke Edith, just off the A438 some ten miles east of Hereford. The builders of the first church there were helped by St. Edith in person, who carried water for the mortar until she sank exhausted to the ground and prayed. In response water flowed out at her feet, thus creating the well. The village may take its name from Queen Edith, widow of Edward the Confessor, rather than St. Edith. Nevertheless, St. Edith's Well was for centuries patronised by people suffering from skin diseases. Some even bathed in its water, to the intense irritation of Lady Foley, the landowner, who in the nineteenth century had a large grille fitted. The well, complete with (open) grille, is on private property beside the entrance to Stoke Edith House.

This was formerly the vicarage but was taken over by the Foleys in 1927 when their own house was destroyed by fire.

Another saint has no well but she has left a considerable impression on Ledbury, only a few miles from Stoke Edith. St. Catherine—a local or unofficial saint—is said to be represented in the form of a late fourteenth-century effigy in the church's clergy vestry, though scholars attribute it to the Pauncefoot or Carew families.

Catherine certainly existed; her signature has even survived on a document dated from Ledbury in 1313. She was born in 1272, the daughter of Sir John Giffard of Brimpsfield, Gloucestershire. She was married at the age of fifteen—not unusual for the time—to Sir Nicholas Audley of Audley, Staffordshire. In 1299 both husband and father died, leaving her between them the castle and town of Llandovery together with estates in Cheshire, Shropshire and Staffordshire. In 1308 she made over some of these lands to her son, Nicholas, in exchange for an annuity of £100. At the same time she may have gone with her other son, Thomas, to live at Hellens in Much Marcle with her cousin by marriage, Yseult Audley.

There, or possibly at Audley Cottage in the same village—to which one story says that she had been ejected from Hellens—Catherine had the revelation that she must seek a town where the bells rang of their own accord, and found a hermitage there. She and her faithful servant, Mabel, duly set off on the quest. Their wanderings included the Sapey Brook, where their horses were stolen, and also Pembridge, Bosbury and finally Ledbury, where the detached

*Ledbury Church as depicted on an old post card*

*Garway Church, where the tower was formerly detached*

towers of the churches are supposed to mark her visit. (Six others in this category in Herefordshire, some of them later joined to their towers—Garway, Holmer, Kington, Richard's Castle, Weobley and Yarpole—do not claim such a connection).

Having arrived close to Ledbury one evening, perhaps after being led there by the trail of the stolen horses, Catherine heard the church bells ringing and sat down on a stone while Mabel went to investigate. Until late in the nineteenth century Cattern's Stone in Cattern's Acre was pointed out to the curious. Catherine's Acre still exists as the name of a house adjacent to the street called Mabel's Furlong. Neither occur in ancient records, so the names are either modern coinages or persisted in oral tradition for many centuries before being written down.

Mabel heard the bells but could see no ringers, perhaps because they were in the detached tower. Even today visitors sometimes look round in puzzlement and ask where the bellringers are. Mabel returned with her good news to Catherine, who set up a hermitage close to the church by one account, perhaps in Audley Cottage which still stands; at Hazle Farm by another—the name was certainly recorded as early as 1086, and the farm supplied Catherine with the 'herbs' (vegetables) and milk on which she lived. A grant registered in 1323 and arranged, we are told, by Yseult Audley, provided the sum of £30 a year on the orders of Edward II towards the expenses of 'the recluse of Ledbury'.

Catherine is often credited with the foundation of St. Catherine's Hospital in Ledbury, but this dates from forty years before she was born, and the dedication was to St. Catherine of Alexandria. Before her death the Ledbury St. Catherine prophesied that should the outer door of her chapel in the church remain closed until it opened of itself the town would become one of the richest in England. However, if human hands intervened it would remain poor. The chapel in question was probably the Chapter House, which may originally have been intended as a shrine to St. Catherine; in the church's own records at one stage it was indeed called St. Catherine's Chapel. The townspeople were careful to keep the door closed till one night some drunken and impious revellers threw it open, thus depriving Ledbury of its potential prosperity.

The date of Catherine's death is not known, but the local saint was remembered for centuries. In 1662 John Jenkins, an eminent musician of the day, composed the tune, *Lady Katharine Audley's Bells*. Visiting friends at Brinsop Court, some 150 years later, William Wordworth wrote:

> When Human touch (as monkish books attest)
> Nor was applied nor could be, Ledbury bells
> Broke forth in concert flung adown the dells,
> And upward, high as Malvern's cloudy crest;
> Sweet tones, and caught by a noble Lady blest
> To rapture. Mabel listened at the side
> Of her loved mistress: soon the music died,
> And Catherine said, HERE I SET UP MY REST.
> Warned in a dream, the Wanderer long had sought
> A home that by such miracle of sound
> Must be revealed: - she heard it now, or felt
> The deep, deep joy of a confiding thought:
> And there, a saintly Anchoress, she dwelt
> Till she exchanged for heaven that happy ground.

In 1834 a Mr. Sanders, the director of a troupe of actors which was visiting Ledbury, decided that a local subject would be good for the box office, and persuaded one of his men, called Macnamara, to write a play. He did so, and *Catherine Audley, or, The Recluse of Ledbury* received 'the greatest approbation' from audiences at the 'Ledbury Theatre' (in fact, the upper room at the Market House). The following year, John Gibbs, junior, of the Homend, published the 92-page

*The Knapp, Ledbury, the birthplace of John Masefield*

text, which now seems to have disappeared without trace. John Masefield, too, has written on 'the Katherine Fable', indulging in the 'harmless pleasure' of believing that the women's heads carved on the arch leading to the chapter house in the church 'are portraits of Katherine and Mabel'.

## Bells

As well as ringing occasionally in a miraculous manner, bells regularly summoned the faithful to prayer. In addition they had a secular role in warning of fire, signalling invasion by an enemy or victory in war. They once announced seedtime, harvest and gleaning. There was even an Oven Bell to proclaim that the lord of the manor's oven was ready to cook his tenants' meat or bread—at a price.

Leominster—and no doubt many other places—had a noon Pancake Bell, on Shrove Tuesday, of course. Goldsmith's famous line, 'The curfew tolls the knell of parting day', was once literally true, since although the legal require-ment ended as early as 1100 the practice continued until relatively recent times. John Masefield, born in Ledbury in 1878, recalled that many parishes still rang the curfew when he was a child. Apart from his own town, Bromyard, Hereford All Saints', Kington, Leominster, Ross and Weobley had a curfew bell.

A much restored plaque on a house near the Riverside Inn at Aymestrey records the dedication of some land in 1515 by William Onneslo to pay for the

sexton to ring a bell daily at 5 a.m. and 8 p.m. between All Saints (1 November) and Candlemas (2 February). The charitable action derived from Onneslo's being led astray, so he claimed, by a will o' the wisp in Poke-house (or Puck-house) Wood, across the River Lugg from the village, one night as he returned home. The bell ringing ceased eventually when the rental of the land raised too small an amount of money. The hole through which the bell rope passed can still be seen in the entrance (which is through the tower) to the church at Aymestrey, to the left of the circular aperture through which the main bell ropes passed. At Eardisley the rental of Bell Rope Acre, as the name indi-

*The plaque to William Onneslo
at Aymestrey*

cates, helped to pay for the upkeep of a vital piece of equipment. Bell Orchard at Pembridge may have had a similar function. Lamp Close at Lucton paid for oil for lighting the church.

'I sing the praise of God, / I sing the woman's knell', says the inscription on a bell at Bosbury. The passing bell indeed gave news of a death in the parish. The practice continued at Kingsland until the Second World War. There, unusually, four rings signified a man, and five a woman, then came as many strokes as the years of his or her age. At Burghill the passing bell tolled before sunset, within twenty-four hours of death, and usually within nine to twelve. Each bell in turn was struck seven times for a man, six for a woman, five for a boy, and four for a girl, after which the tenor bell was rung as many times as the deceased's years. At Lugwardine the sexton received 1s. for 'passing the death bell'. He also announced to parishioners that a funeral was over by tolling one of the bells twenty or thirty times.

Inscriptions on the bells reinforced their message of mortality. 'For the living I do call, / To the grave I summon all', occurs in at least fifteen Herefordshire churches, including Leintwardine, sometimes with variations. 'Prosperity to this parish' (or 'place') and 'Peace and Good Neighbourhood' were other widely favoured inscriptions. A stern warning recurs at Bosbury with:

> All men that hear my roing [?roaring] sound,
> Repent before ye lye in ground.

The varied number and pitch of bells in different churches produced different patterns of sound which in turn were adapted into jingles, often irreverent. 'Roast beef and old perry, / Say the bells of Bosbury' compares with:

> There is pudding in the pot,
> All stuck with plums,
> All stuck with plums,
> As big as my two thumbs,
> Say the bells of Winforton.

In allusion to meagre crops produced by the poor soil of the locality, the two bells of Welsh Newton allegedly repeated 'Erfen, cawl erfen'—turnip, turnip soup. On the other hand, Weston-under-Penyard boasted 'Stick a goose and dress un say the bells of Wesson'. More humbly, 'Buttermilk and whey, / Say the bells of Garway'. Slightly bizarre is 'An old man with a blue beard, / Say the bells of Bromyard'; and people at Staunton-on-Wye claimed that the bells of Norton Canon said: 'Norton's men be hungry, / Stole a pig last Thursday'. There are many more examples of such popular inventiveness.

Eastnor people judged the weather by the sound of their neighbours' bells:

> Bromesberrow rings in summer sweet,
> But Coller [Colwall] sounds for snow.
> Ledbury chimes for rain and heat;
> If Donn'ton's heard, 'twill blow.

The ringers themselves could be irreverent or indisciplined. Several bell chambers—at Cradley, Kingsland, Mathon, Leominster and Weobley, for example—have or had (some have been removed or whitewashed over) inscribed tablets or painted boards with lists of rules and penalties, sometimes cast into rhyme. One set, from Cradley, dates from the eighteenth century:

> Ye Gentlemen Ringers both far and near,
> That are disposed for to Ring here;
> Observe this law, and mark it well,
> The Man that Overthrows his Bell;
> Sixpence he to the Clark must pay
> Before that he go hence away,
> If he ring with Glove, Spur, or Hat,
> Sixpence he must pay for that:
> If he either Curse, or Swear,
> Six-pence must pay while you are here,
> This is not a place to Quarrel in.
> To Curse and Swear it is a Sin.

(Overthrowing a bell, caused by too strong a pull, puts it out of action after breaking a restraining stave).

Similar verses, dating from 1819, were to be seen in the ringing chamber at Mathon in the 1990s (and are probably still there):

> You ringers all that do ring here
> Ring carefully with hand and ear
> Let every one observe his bell
> To ring it right and rule it well
> For 'tis indeed a shame to him
> That takes a bell and cannot ring
> It's better for him to stand off
> Than that should men at him laugh
> For he that interrupts a peal
> Shall surely pay a quart of ale
> Or ring with glove spur or hat
> Must pay the like be sure of that
> These rules lets all observe and use

That neither bells nor ropes abuse
In silent order play your part
For ringing is the best of art.

A more general poem, inscribed at Leominster in about 1700, was removed in the mid-nineteenth century during alterations to the south arch of the western tower of the priory church:

If you'll give eare, then you shall heare
of ringing in commendation;
Of our bonny bells with their shuger'd knells,
Which are held in admiration.
Our ancestors in ringing, took this order,
1, 2, 3, 4, 5, 6, 7, they never taught us further.
To rays, to fall, to close withal,
It was their whole intention;
Nothing did change, they thought it strange,
They knew no such invention.
But as in trades and arts new things are daily learned,
Those noble spirited hearts their ringing have decerned.
Such pretty parts, such setts, such tunes,
And such several notes of change!
--- in his place,
From music he is estranged.
The pleasant hills and dales, the mounts, the hom, the meadows,
Attend unto our tales the groves and dainty shadows.
The evening's rill deplores then still, with late and early;
Peace, boys, and speak not a word: let us hear our bells go clearly.
Each one attend, they doe as commend,
And think it so very strange,
When that they heare our bells strike so cleare,
And at every pull a change.
Churchwardens, we you pray, keep these our bells in order,
And careful always be our music still to further.
So newly strung, with cottrell [? washer] fast and cotter,
Let beme and wheels be joyn'd well, that we have no totter.

George Wargent of Ledbury, born in 1824 and writing in 1905, recollected:

It was the custom in the belfry then to have the ringers' jar or barrel, this consisted of 4 1/2 gallons of beer or cider, which was trammed on one of the steps in the ringing chamber and after a peal, a horn of beer or cider was handed round to each ringer. It was supposed in those days that the ringing went better if intoxicating liquors were handed round.

Once the bell ringers had called parishioners to church another team of musicians took over: a band provided accompaniment for the choir and congregation before the days when organs became universal. Thomas Hardy in *Under the Greenwood Tree* has left an affectionate portrait of a 'quire' of village musicians just before they were displaced by an organ. J.A. La Trobe, curate of St. Peter's, Hereford, criticised even organists for their 'frivolous taste' and lamented that 'much impropriety' was caused by admitting women to church choirs. Writing in 1831 he objected to singers' 'want of reverence in the House of God', 'fondness for display', 'obstinate rejection of advice' and 'bad taste'.

Many churches banished musicians from the chancel to a gallery, usually positioned at the west end. Clodock still has one; as does Kilpeck. At St. Margaret's Church in the village of the same name in the Golden Valley the richly-carved rood loft—still in existence, and described by Pevsner as 'one of the wonders of Herefordshire'—was used by singers and musicians alike, and also doubled as a school room. Later, village bands gave way to organists, initially still positioned in the west gallery but then moved to the nave or chancel. An intermediate stage in some churches was filled by a barrel organ programmed to play hymn tunes and powered by a hand-turned crank. At Bosbury barrels have been preserved which played eleven tunes, including *Rockingham*, *Melcombe* and *Stuttgart*.

Choir outings and Sunday School treats were a commonplace part of the church calendar until at least the mid-twentieth century. At Lugwardine the choir and bellringers enjoyed an annual dinner in the village's old parish room:

> It was a real good meal, too. A large piece of beef was placed at the head of the table, and at the other end a large piece of mutton or pork. The Vicar carved the beef, and Mr Ted Brooks, the local pig-butcher, the mutton or pork. (It is worth mentioning that Mr Brooks was a ringer at the church for over fifty years). Each year Brooks always had the same request from the Vicar, 'Will you please sharpen the carving knife?' The meal was always a real good hot one, cooked and served by the servant girls of the vicarage. The regular staff there consisted of cook, parlourmaid and housemaid.
>
> The Vicar usually left the gathering at about 10 pm. Someone then produced a jar each of ale and cider, kindly donated by one of the local inns [Crown and Anchor and New Inn] and a farmer.

The vicar mentioned was Rev. A.C. Lee (incumbent 1884-1920), and the recollection came from Fred Arrowsmith.

## Epitaphs

Village musicians sometimes have memorials in churchyards. Harps are depicted on the gravestone at Bridstow of Thomas Smith, landlord of the Anchor Inn (now a private house called Upper Orchard) at Hoarwithy in the late eighteenth century. Members of other trades and professions had fitting inscriptions. A verse traditional to blacksmiths is found at Eardisley, Richard's Castle and Ledbury. The last, to Thomas Russell, 'Blacksmith of this town ... who died 24th may 1838', now suffers from erosion, but read:

> My Sledge and Hammer lie reclined.
> My Bellows too have lost their wind.
> My Fire's extinct my Forge decayed.
> And in the dust my Vice is laid.
> My Coal is spent, my Iron gone,
> My Nails are drove my work is done.
> My fire-dried corpse now lies at rest.
> My soul smoke-like is soaring to the blest.

A trainer of fighting cocks, John Andrews, who died in 1799, is remembered at Peterchurch:

> Alas, poor Captain, winged by cruel death,
> He pecked in vain, o'ermatched, resigned his breath,
> Lov'd social mirth, none dare his word distrust,
> Sincere in friendship, and was truly just.

*John Abel's tomb at Sarnesfield*

John Abel, 'the King's Carpenter', died in 1674, and was buried at Sarnesfield. He built handsome half-timbered market houses at Brecon, Kington, Ledbury and Leominster (of which only the last two survive). His tomb shows the tools of his trade—rule, compasses and square—and bears these lines:

> This craggy stone a covering is for an
>     Architector's bed;
> That lofty buildings raised high, yet
>     now lyes low his head;
> His line and rule, so death concludes,
>     are locked up in store;
> Build they who list,
> Or they who wist,
> For he can build no more.
> His house of clay could hold no longer,
> May Heaven's joy frame him a
>     stronger.

The state of relationship between married couples is reflected in epitaphs such as the peremptory farewell from Thomas Weston to his first wife at Bredwardine: 'Here lies my wife; here let her lie; / Now she's at rest, and so am I'. At Eaton Bishop Richard and Margaret Snead, who both died in 1678, have a joint epitaph:

> One bed we shared; one tomb now holds us,
> And our bones, mingled with dust now lie together.
> One death was ours; one year took us away.
> One day saved us and gave us back to God.

The writers of epitaphs were not above making puns when the opportunity arose. Even eminent people were not exempt. Theophilus Field was successively bishop of Llandaff, St. David's and Hereford. When he died in 1636 this epitaph was deemed appropriate:

> The Sun that light unto three Churches gave
> Is set; this Field is buried in a grave,
> This Sun shall rise, this Field renew his flowers,
> The sweetness breathe for age, not for hours.

*The detached tower at Bosbury Church*

Still in Hereford Cathedral, the fourteenth-century Swinfield tomb shows little pigs on a green background—hence, swine field.

At times the dead set out by means of their epitaphs to address the living from beyond the grave. Not surprisingly, the mood is inclined to be grim. 'Remember' cries Thomas Barrett (who died in 1747 at the age of 23) from a tablet fixed outside the south wall of the nave at Bosbury:

> Remember, all you who pass this way,
> As you are now so once was I,
> And as I am so will you be,
> Therefore prepare to follow me.

Almost the same words occur at St. Mary's, Kington, and no doubt else-where. Similar sentiments are conveyed in another traditional verse which crops up at Mathon (for John Barrett, to the left of the porch):

> All you that come my grave to see
> As I am now so must you be;
> Repent in time, make no delay,
> I in my prime was snatched away.
> In love I liv'd, in peace I died,
> My life was ask'd—but God denied.

Margaret Jones who died in 1805 has sombre words on a tablet in the chancel of Clodock Church:

> Oft by the silent grave I once did tread,
> Mused on the short memorials of the dead,
> Thou too, that readest this must lie supine
> Whilst others read some epitaph of time.

This was for a baby who died at Kingsland in 1683:

> So young and so soon dead, conclude we may
> She was too good longer on earth to stay.

The same kind of hope is expressed at Upton Bishop on the north wall of the nave for a woman who died in 1698, aged 29:

> Here lies interr'd from Nature's Flesh and Blood,
> Being taken in her prime, Susannah Underwood,
> Death sunk her Body from on Earth to Rest
> Her soule, I hope, sings Hallelujahs with the Blest.

Similarly confident—perhaps too confident—is the epitaph to Sir Robert Weaver (died 1728, aged 70) in the sanctuary at Aymestrey Church:

> This modest Stone, which few vain Marbles can
> May truly say: here lys a worthy Man,
> Foe to contention, Freind [sic] to harmless ease,
> Content he liv'd, within the Arms of Peace,
> Gentle to the poor, respectful to the Great
> To Kindred tender and to Equals Sweet
> Calmly he look'd on either Life or here
> Saw nothing to regrett or there to fear
> But dyd submissive unto Naturs Law

In strong assurance whilst pleas'd Angels Strove
Gently to guard him to the Bless'd above.

Other inscriptions confined themselves to the minimum detail, such as this cast-iron slab, one of several outside the east window of the remote church at Burrington:

HEERLIETH RO
BERT STEWARD
WHOE DECESED
THE 17 OF IANVARY
1619
ETATISSVAE 52
(*aetatis suae* — at the age of).

An epitaph seen by H.J. Massingham at Abbey Dore is dismissive of both epitaph writers and readers:

Reader pass on, not waste your time
On bad biography, and much worse rhyme.
For what I am this cumbrous clay immures,
And what I was is no concern of yours.

*One of the many cast-iron gravestones outside the east window at Burrington Church*

## Churchyards

Despite their many gloomy associations churchyards were often used for recreation. At Craswall a levelled area by the north wall of the church was used for playing fives, and a hollow beyond as a pit for cockfighting. A stone bench along the outside of the chancel accommodated spectators. At St. Margaret's, where fives was played against the north wall of the nave, the hinges of shutters which protected the east window can still be seen. A tell-tale painted line for fives can still be made out on the church tower at Burghill. 'The remains of their [villagers'] wakes and Sunday sports', wrote Rev. John Webb, 'have not been entirely abandoned in our own times; and almost every old church tower till of late bore the red line of the fives' court where the youths were accustomed to play'. At St. Mary's, Kington, the annual wake held on the Sunday of or following 15 August in the churchyard lasted until 1795.

Various oddities are also found in churchyards. A two-ton mass of rock at Bosbury, thought to have been 'held in veneration in heathen times', said a nineteenth-century clergyman, was buried beneath a cross, presumably to nullify its malevolent influence. Then for some reason it was dug up in 1796 and moved to its present position on the south side of the tower. At Ashperton an old font now in the churchyard perhaps served for the christening of Katharine Grandison whose name has been linked with the origin of the Order of the Garter. It was she who dropped her garter at a court ball and had it retrieved by Edward III. His famous comment—*Honi soit qui mal y pense*, (shame to him who thinks ill of it)—has been attributed to a desire not to spare Katharine's blushes but to shield her from a possible accusation of sorcery. The suggestion, based on the notion that the garter was somehow a witch's badge at the time, seems rather fanciful. Daniel Defoe in his *Tour through the Whole Island of Great Britain* mentions the monument in Worcester Cathedral to the Countess of Salisbury (Katherine's married name) 'who dancing before, or with King Edward III in his great hall at Windsor, dropped her garter, which the king taking up, honoured it so much as to make it the denominating ensign for his new order of knighthood'. *The Dictionary of National Biography* calls the story 'palpably fictitious', and points out that its first source, Polydore Vergil, visited England 150 years after the Order of the Garter was set up.

The devil's head is seen by some in the small finely worked bronze door-knocker at Dormington Church. The large ring hanging from the grimacing mouth may have secured sanctuary for any outlaw who could manage to grasp it. The original, which dates from the twelfth century, was stolen in 1980 and recovered only by a fortunate chance. Since then it has been kept in a museum, with only a copy remaining in its place. It has been suggested that the art of the metal worker who made the original knocker had a strong influence on the stone carvers who perfected their work at Shobdon, Kilpeck and elsewhere in what became known as the Herefordshire School of romanesque sculpture.

*The knocker on the door of Dormington Church*

Until 1811, when it disappeared during the course of rebuilding, a large green dragon could be seen painted on the west wall of Mordiford Church. The beast shown was in fact probably a wyvern from the arms of the priory of St. Guthlac, which held the living of Mordiford. Thomas Blount of Orleton described it in 1679 as being twelve feet long, with four legs, webbed feet, a long tail and two griffin-like wings. A local poet, writing in 1847, asked:

> Who has not heard, of Herefordian birth,
> Who has not heard, as winter evenings lag on,
> That tale of awe to some—to some of mirth,
> Of Mordiford's most famous, huge, Green Dragon?

One explanation of the figure's origin claimed that Mordred, nephew of King Arthur, forded the River Wye, thus giving the name of Mordred's Ford, and hence, Mordiford (though official etymology prefers 'great house ford'). As a result he won a battle and deposited the defeated pary's banner with its green dragon emblem in the nearby church. When the standard eventually faded away the device was painted on the church wall. A chronological problem is that the earliest fragments of the present building are twelfth century, and therefore many hundreds of years later than Mordred, even if he existed.

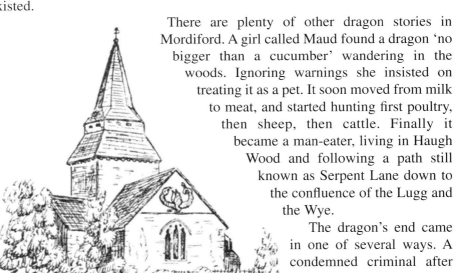

There are plenty of other dragon stories in Mordiford. A girl called Maud found a dragon 'no bigger than a cucumber' wandering in the woods. Ignoring warnings she insisted on treating it as a pet. It soon moved from milk to meat, and started hunting first poultry, then sheep, then cattle. Finally it became a man-eater, living in Haugh Wood and following a path still known as Serpent Lane down to the confluence of the Lugg and the Wye.

The dragon's end came in one of several ways. A condemned criminal after being offered his life as a reward hacked it to pieces while it slept; or hid in a cider barrel by the river and killed it by firing a gun through the bunghole.

*A drawing of Mordiford Church c.1808, showing the dragon painted on the west wall*

Alternatively the dragon impaled itself on a knife-studded barrel from which the man emerged to administer the *coup de grâce*. The three stories unite in saying that the criminal failed to enjoy his triumph because he died from the after-effects of the dragon's noxious breath. A further twist is provided by the notion that the unfortunate hero was no outlaw, but a member of the respected Garston family. Yet another suggestion is that the villagers of Mordiford combined to hack the dragon to death as it slept off the effects of gorging itself on a drowned ox washed down the river. As late as 1875 the rector found two old women trying to drown a couple of newts in the font lest they grow up to renew the scourge. In 1973 to celebrate the centenary of their school local children staged a pageant showing a battle between green and red dragons which ended when the red dragon went to the west to become the symbol of Wales while the green dragon became the picture on the church.

Carved dragons feature in churches at Kilpeck and Shobdon. At Brinsop a dragon writhes in its death throes at the feet of St. George on a twelfth-century tympanum in the church dedicated to him. The encounter was believed to have taken place locally, in a field to the north of the church called Lower Stanks; and to the south in Duck's Pool Meadow is the Dragon's Well. However, scholars tell us that although it was executed by Herefordshire craftsmen the sculpture's theme derives from a carving at Parthenay-le-Vieux in western France.

The tiny church at Kilpeck has a wealth of carvings, many of them Norman, both inside and out. Some eighty figures on corbels include real and imaginary birds and beasts, a strange creature playing an unrecognisable instrument, a kilted dancer, and two lovers embracing. Some are missing; they probably showed naked men in a state of arousal. Asked in the 1920s about damage to one figure an old man replied: 'Ah, that wur Miss - - -. A never could suffer that un, so a get her a pole and a pothered un off.' One wonders what the lady thought of the female figure on the south side of the apse, which represents a woman holding open her genitals.

*The sheila-na-gig corbel at Kilpeck Church*

This is a sheila-na-gig—meaning 'am immodest woman', a figure which inspires extensive speculation. A Celtic earth mother who gives life and death; a Norman joke carried out by masons in a period of artistic licence when the decorative features of churches covered a wide range of subject matter; 'the witch on the wall'; 'a powerful female protector'; merely 'a quaint representation of the human figure': these are some of the theories. Only 18 examples of such figures are known in Britain, scattered all over the country. Many clergymen would prefer them not to be there but accept them as part of the fabric of their churches. Some people feel differently, and there was a tradition that a young man would take his bride-to-be and introduce her to the sheila so that their marriage would be blessed with plenty of children.

## Object lessons

Within churches, too, are many items which express popular beliefs or have given rise to them. A favourite motif is the foliate head or green man, which some say symbolises sadness and sacrifice, death and ruin; others life and renewal, a potent force erupting from the collective subconscious. (The Green Man of inn signs is probably the Jack-in-the-Green of a spring ritual which dates back only to the eighteenth century). There are examples of foliate heads carved in stone in the churches at Garway, Leominster, Rowlstone, Much Marcle (christianised by the addition of a cross on a chain round the neck), Bosbury (on the Harford tomb, dating from 1579), Dore Abbey (on a fallen roof boss) and no doubt elsewhere. A good specimen is carved on a door lintel in Hereford Cathedral.

The green man is sometimes found in wood on misericords, wooden brackets fixed to the underside of choirstall seats so as to give support to singers standing through the long services. Carvings in such a lowly position seem to have been left to the fantasy of craftsmen, so we find not only Biblical scenes but fabulous beasts, traditional sports, rough humour and vignettes from everyday life.

Hereford Cathedral contains some 60 misericords. They include a naked man seated on horseback facing the tail. Among other offences forgery was punished in this way, and one instance is to be found in the Hereford records for 1535.

*Green Man carved on a corbel of the chancel arch at Garway Church*

*A pair of wrestlers on a misericord from Wigmore Abbey, now at Leintwardine*

Misericords found elsewhere include subjects as diverse as two mermaids (All Saints', Hereford), a fox running away with a goose (Canon Pyon), and a battered pair of wrestlers (Leintwardine, originally from Wigmore Abbey).

A fifteenth-century carving—not a misericord—at All Saints' Church in Hereford aroused controversy in 1998 when a proposal by the vicar and parochial church council to sell postcard and fibreglass reproductions was voted down by the congregation. The figure, high in the rafters but brought closer and spotlit with the installation of a mezzanine floor for a café, shows a man exposing himself and is affectionately known as Seamus O'Toole or Wee Willie Winkie. It may represent a master mason caricatured by craftsmen because he had failed to pay their wages on time, or possibly at all.

Items in churches are usually rather more orthodox. In St. Peter's Church at Peterchurch on the inside wall over the south door is a carp with a golden chain round its neck. An old man told Parson Kilvert in 1876:

> They do say the fish was first seen at Dorstone and speared there, but he got away and they hunted him down to Peterchurch and killed him close by the church. He was as big as a salmon and had a gold chain round his neck. They do say you can see the blood now upon the stones at Dorstone where the fish was speared first.

*Medieval carving at All Saints' Church, Hereford*

The Golden Well at Dorstone where the fish was first seen is the source of the River Dore, which then flows down to Peterchurch and beyond. Peterchurch had its own well, consecrated supposedly by St. Peter himself, who dropped in the fish with the golden chain which was to live there for ever.

Funerary monuments have given rise to unofficial commentaries of various kinds. At Edvin Ralph a tablet to Maud de Edefen dating from about 1325 bears an inscription promising 60 days' pardon from the bishop of Hereford to those saying a *paternoster* and an *ave* for her. A local tradition already in existence in 1656 holds that Maud was loved by the lords of both Edvin Ralph and nearby Edvin Loach. As they fought over her she rushed between their swords and was mortally wounded. The two fenced on until they both fell dead.

At Much Cowarne the mutilated effigy of a knight dating from the thirteenth century is considered to be that of Grimbald de Pauncefoot. A second figure, now lost, represented his wife, Constance, whom he married in 1251. Its left arm missing above the wrist was taken to demonstrate 'memory and confirmation' of the lady's 'heroic conduct'. When Grimbald was captured on crusade Saladin demanded as ransom 'a joint of his wyffe'. When she received the news, Constance, living up to her name, summoned a surgeon from Gloucester Priory, had her hand removed, and sent it to North Africa to secure her husband's release.

Strangely enough, two other Pauncefoot wives suffered in a similar way for their husbands. Sybil, commemorated in effigy at Crickhowell, ransomed another crusader by giving up her her right hand. Dorothy was merely betrothed to Richard Pauncefoot of Hasfield in Gloucestershire when he was captured by Barbary pirates. To the sultan's daughter, who wished him to marry her, he said 'My lady in England is faithful and true, why she'd give her right hand for me'.

*St. Weonard's Church as shown on a post card in the 1970s*

*A south-east view of Upton Bishop as drawn in the nineteenth century*

were excommunicated by the bishop of Hereford, but there is no record that they were ever brought to justice.

A less terminal misadventure overtook Rev. John Jackson of Ledbury when he was suspended in 1869 after rumours—started, apparently, by the local doctor—went round the town that he had fathered illegitimate children. Two years later a church enquiry exonerated and reinstated him. Parishioners who declined to believe him innocent set up an alternative church in a hut in New Street which became known as the tin tabernacle. They refused even to allow themselves to be buried by Jackson, and arranged for their funerals to take place at Eastnor. It is possible that in 1878 John Masefield's family had him baptised at Preston Church, some three miles away, because doubts still lingered about Jackson. The unfortunate clergyman found himself pilloried in a London street ballad, *The Frolicsome parson Outwitted*, and also in a song which circulated orally for the best part of a century, *The Ledbury Parson*, which runs in part:

> In Ledbury town in Herefordshire
> They rucked up a row, with the parson there.
> This pious gentleman, so they say,
> Was far too fond of going astray,

(Chorus )
And if going astray should be your plan,
Just think of the Ledbury clergyman.

This pious gentleman, you all know,
Did a very religious example show.
'Stead of teaching the folks to preach and pray
He was kissing and cuddling night and day.

*Jackson's pulpit*

This parson he was a roving blade,
He courted the cook and the servant maid,
Gave out his text and winked his eye:
'Come kiss me, girls, and multiply'.

Well they summoned him up and made him pay
One half a crown a week, they say;
So clergymen my warning take
Or you'll suffer the Ledbury parson's fate.

In fact, Jackson continued in office at Ledbury until his death in 1891. An elaborate pulpit which he carved himself over a period of seven years can still be seen in the church. His career overlapped with that of Rev. William Poole, vicar at Hoarwithy from 1854 until 1901. Poole was a monied eccentric who unlike many of his colleagues defended hiring fairs (see chapter 7). He had a school built at Hoarwithy, provided houses, and paid for the church to be transformed into the Italianate structure which is still much admired. If at the end of a week he found the work done on the church to be unsatisfactory, he would draw the wages in farthings (coins worth a quarter of an old penny) and throw them down the steep flight of steps leading from the road, where the men had to scramble for them.

Rumours (in the case of Jackson) and spiteful actions (in the case of Poole) of this sort often outweighed churchmen's philanthrophy in the public eye, and a fund of anti-clericalism existed which produced items like *The Parson's Ode* from a manuscript in a Ledbury family scrapbook (with punctuation as in the original):

Money! oh Money, thy praises I sing
Thou art my Saviour, my God and King.
'Tis for thee, that I preach, and for thee that I pray
And make a collection twice each sabbath day.

I have candles, and all sorts of dresses to buy
For I wish you to know my church is called high
I don't mean in structure of steeple or wall
But so high that the Lord cannot reach it at all

I have poor in my parish who need some relief
I preach to their poverty, and pay for their grief
I send my box round to to them morning and night
And hope they'll remember the poor widow's mite

I gather my knowledge from wisdom's great tree
And the whole of my trinity's £. S. D.

Pounds, shillings & pence are all that I crave
From my first step on earth, to the brink of the grave

And when I'm laid low, and my body at rest
Place a box on my grave, 'tis my latest request
That friends may all see, who came for reflection
I can't rest in peace without a collection

Money's my creed, I'll not pray without it
My heavens is closed against all those who doubt it
For this is the essence of parsons' religion
Come regular to church, and be plucked like a pigeon.

## Customs

As well as the normal seasonal celebrations churches sometimes have (or had) their own traditional observances. On Plough Sunday (nearest to 6 January) ploughs used to be blessed in churches. Places where this happened include Kimbolton and nearby Leominster, where a plough was kept in the Priory

Church. On the nearest Sunday to Candlemas Day (2 February) small loaves known as Garrold's Bread are still blessed in the church at Aston Ingham and distributed to parishioners under the terms of a bequest made in 1859 by Richard Garrold. The pax (peace) cakes given out on Palm Sunday (the week before Easter) at Hentland, King's Caple and Sellack, derive from other legacies. The practice apparently started at Sellack after Thomas More, a priest who owned land there provided in his will—drawn up on Palm Sunday, 1484, the day before he died—for an annual distribution to parishioners of cakes and

*Distribution of pax cakes at King's Caple* ale costing a total of 6s 8d

64

*Good Friday distribution of bread at Aymestrey*

'for the good of my soul' (meaning, presumably, that the beneficiaries would pray for him). A further bequest in 1570 by Lady Scudamore may have extended the custom to one of the other parishes. The pax cakes, now made at a Peterstow bakery, are round shortbread biscuits stamped with the likeness of a paschal lamb and the words 'Peace and Good Neighbourhood'. The distribution, after morning service on Palm Sunday, has by no means been uninterrupted since mediaeval times, but it is remarkable in continuing at all.

In a custom once shared with neighbouring Wales, Herefordshire people once decked the graves of deceased relatives with flowers on Palm Sunday. The flowering later moved to Easter Saturday and continued at Ross and Hereford until at least the mid-1970s. At Easter women were expected to wear a new hat to church. Eggs, an emblem of fertility, were once donated to churches at Easter, presumably to swell the funds. Some ground rents were paid in this form. The chocolate Easter eggs of today are an unconscious link with this past.

Forty days after Easter comes Ascension Day, and this is preceded by the four days—Sunday to Wednesday—of Rogationtide. From the eighth century onwards blessings were asked at Rogationtide (the Latin *rogare*, means to ask) on the coming corn harvest and the beating of bounds—otherwise called processioning or bannering—took place. The parson would lead his parish-ioners round their boundaries, taking up his station to read from the Bible by strategic trees which came to be called Gospel Oak (for example, where the parishes of Kingsland, Lucton, Aymestrey and Shobdon meet; and at Eastnor, marking the boundary with Ledbury parish) or Gospel Yew (Bosbury, Castle Frome and Canon Frome). Sometimes the processions carried branches of trees which were stuck in the ground and occasionally took root. Other landmarks were stones (called liberty, or mere-stones), wells, and even public houses.

Boys were beaten, bumped or ducked, or given buns or pennies for which to scramble, all to impress the boundaries on their minds so that they could testify to them for the rest of their lives if the need arose. For adult, eating and drinking were important parts of the proceedings, as we know from many records which have survived.

Such perambulations continued at Hereford until 1890, where proceedings began with a trip down the Wye in boats to the Franchise Stone, then across fields to another stone, and from there along Holy Well Gutter to the Cock at Tupsley. Next the walkers went to Baynton Wood, Lugg Meadows, Lugg Bridge, where an omnibus took them to Holmer, Three Elms and a particular cottage at Stretton Sugwas. The first day's march ended at the river bank oppo-site the stone on the Hunderton side. On the second day the party set off from the stone near the river to another near Hunderton fold-yard, and then on to St. John's parish boundary marker. The ceremony ended at its starting point by the Wye opposite the Whalebone Inn at Eign. The total distance covered was $17\frac{1}{4}$ miles.

In recent years certain parishes have shown an interest in reviving some form of bound beating. In celebration of the millennium Colwall churchgoers decided to revive a tradition. The *Malvern Gazette* reported:

> Organizers have put together a route that will take residents on a 13-mile walk around Colwall's boundary, or as close as they can safely get, and they plan to integrate times of praise and reflection and provide some fun on the village green.
>
> The walk begins at St James's Church at 10 am on Sunday, May 21, and takes walkers to Oyster Hill and Evendine Corner and from there up to the Malvern Hills Hotel. From there, they will cross the Hills to the Wyche Cutting and then take the path back down to St James's Church, hopefully arriving back at 6.30 pm.

In Hereford Cathedral the ceremony of the Boy Bishop, which dates back to the thirteenth century, is held during a special service on the nearest Saturday to St. Nicholas' Day (6 December). The custom is intended as a special cele-bration of St. Nicholas, the patron saint of children (and also of sailors, unmar-ried women, merchants, pawnbrokers, apothecaries and perfumiers). After

*Timothy Sarsons, the Boy Bishop for 1991*

receiving the real bishop's blessing the boy he has chosen from among the choristers, dressed in full episcopal rig, replaces him on his throne as the choir sings 'He hath put down the mighty from their seat'. Hereford is one of a very few places where this ceremony survives. The Boy Bishop remains in office, taking part in all services—except, of course, those requiring an ordained priest—until Holy Innocents' Day or Childermas (28 December). Because of its associations—this was the occasion when Herod's massacre of male infants took place—the day was considered particularly unlucky. No work was started on it, nor new clothes donned for the first time. Fortunately, any gloom would soon be lifted by the imminent New Year celebrations.

# CHAPTER 4

# Lives

As they always will be, the beginning and end of life are marked by rites of passage and attended by many beliefs. Within the poles of existence lies the magnetic field of relationships between the sexes, another fruitful source of traditions. A great many methods of divination—now almost wholly abandoned—were employed by young women in an effort to discover the identity of their future partners. Marriage, still a major time for family celebration, was and is surrounded by customs. The poor man's practice of wife selling has long been superseded by relatively easy procedures for legal divorce, not to speak of the widespread current habit of couples' living together or separating without benefit of clergy or legal process. Certain rituals of communal disapproval of individual morality, such as 'colestaff' or 'skimmington', have also disappeared though they might be overdue for revival.

## Birth

In Herefordshire there was a notion that the father of a child suffered as much during its gestation and birth as the mother. Thus, if a woman refused to identify the father of an illegitimate child people would watch to see which young man was taken ill at the time of her delivery.

It was considered unlucky—tempting fate, perhaps—to bring a child's cradle into the house before the birth. A cradle previously there would be stored elsewhere from the beginning of the pregnancy. A new cradle was unlucky in any case, so an old one would be handed down from generation to generation, usually on the male side. As cradles fell out of use the superstitions associated with them passed to cots, and even prams.

To help a woman in labour sheep's lights were tied with string to her hands and feet, or a roasted mouse was laid on her stomach. To help ease the pain of childbirth women, until the early twentieth century, bought a sheet which they called *Our Saviour's Letter* to hang over the bed. One version of this was printed in Hereford (see overleaf) in about 1908.

# A Copy of a Letter,

### WRITTEN

## By Our Saviour JESUS CHRIST.

Found 18 Miles from *Iconium*, 65 Years after our blessed Saviour's Crucifixion: Transmitted from the holy City by a converted Jew, faithfully translated from the Original Hebrew Copy, now in the Possession of the Lady *Cuba's* Family at

*Mesopotamia*. This Letter was written by *Jesus Christ*, and found under a great Stone both round and large, at the Foot of the Cross, near a Village called *Mesopotamia*. Upon the Stone was written or engraven—*Blessed is he that shall turn me over.*

People that saw it prayed to God earnestly, and desired he would make known to them the Meaning of this Writing, that they might not attempt in vain to turn it over. In the mean Time there came a little Child about six or seven Years old, and turned it over, which I am without any Help or Assistance, to the Admiration of all those that stood by. And under this Stone was found this Letter which was written by Jesus Christ, and was carried to the City of Iconium, and there published by a Person belonging to the Cuba Family; and in the Letter was written the Commandments of Jesus Christ, signed by the Angel Gabriel, 78 Years after our Saviour's Birth. To which are added, King Agbarus's Letter to our Saviour and our Saviour's Answer; Also his Miracles, and Lentulus's Epistle to the Senate of Rome.

### A Letter of Jesus Christ.

WHOSOEVER worketh on the Sabbath-Day shall be cursed. I command you to go to the Church, and keep the Lord's-Day holy, without doing any Manner of Work. You shall not idly spend your Time with bedecking yourself with superfluities of costly Apparel and vain Dresses, for I have ordained a Day of Rest. I will have that Day kept holy that your Sins may be forgiven you. You shall not break my Commandments, but observe and keep them, written with my own Hand and spoken with my own Mouth. You shall not only go to Church yourself, but your Men Servants and Maid Servants, and observe my Words and learn my Commandments. You shall finish your Labour every Saturday Afternoon by six o'clock, at which hour the Preparation of the Sabbath begins. I advise you to fast five Fridays in every Year, beginning with Good Friday, and to continue the four Fridays immediately following, in Remembrance of the five bloody Wounds which I received for all Mankind. You shall diligently and peaceably labour in your respective Callings, wherein it hath pleased God to call you. You shall love one another with brotherly Love, and cause them that are baptized to come to Church and receive the Sacrament of the Lord's Supper; and be made Members of the Church: In so doing I will give you a long Life, many Blessings, your Land shall flourish, and your Cattle shall bring forth in Abundance and I will give you many Blessings and Comforts in the greatest Temptations: and he that doth to the contrary shall be unprofitable. I will also send a Hardness of Heart upon them, till I see them; but especially upon the impenitent Unbelievers: He that hath given to the Poor shall not be unprofitable. Remember to keep holy the Sabbath-Day, for the Seventh Day I have taken to rest myself; and he that hath a Copy of this Letter, written with my own Hand, and spoken with my own Mouth, and keepeth it without publishing it to others, shall not prosper; but he that publisheth it to others shall be blessed of me. And though his sins be in Number as the Stars of the Sky, and he believes in this, he shall be pardoned; and if he believes not this Writing and this Commandment; I will send my Plagues upon him, and consume both him, his Children, and his Cattle. And whosoever shall have a Copy of this Letter, written with my own Hand, and keep it in their own Houses nothing shall hurt them, neither Pestilence, Lightning, nor Thunder shall do them any Hurt. And if a Woman be with Child, and in Labour, and a Copy of this Letter be about her, and she firmly puts her Trust in me, she shall be safely delivered of her Birth. You shall have no News of me but by the Holy Scriptures, until the Day of Judgment.

All Goodness and Prosperity shall be on the House where a Copy of this Letter shall be found.

### Christ's *Cures and Miracles.*

HE cleansed a Leper by only touching him. He healed the Centurion's Servant that was afflicted with a Fever. Several possessed with Devils. A violent Tempest was stilled by him. A man sick of the Palsy. Raised a Maid from the Dead. He cured two blind Men. A dumb Man possessed of the Devil. He fed above five Thousand with five Loaves and two Fishes. He walked on the Sea. All the Diseases in Genesaret he healed by the Touch of his Garment. He cured a Woman vexed with a Devil, and a Multitude that were lame, blind, dumb, maimed, etc. He fed above four Thousand with four Loaves and a few little Fishes.

### King Agbarus's *Letter to our Saviour.*

I Have heard of thee, and of the Cures wrought by thee without Herbs or Medicines: For it is reported thou re-storest Sight unto the blind, makest the Lame to walk, cleansest the Leprous, raisest the Dead, and healest those who are tormented with Diseases of a long Continuance.

Having heard all this of thee, I was fully persuaded to believe one of these Things, either that thou art a very God, and camest down from Heaven to do such Miracles; or else thou art the Son of God, and performest them. Wherefore I have now sent these lines, entreating thee to come hither, and cure my Disease; besides, having heard that the Jews murmur against thee, and contrive to do thee a Mischief, I invite thee to my City, which is a little one indeed, but beautiful, and sufficient to entertain us both.

### Our SAVIOUR'S *Answer.*

BLESSED art thou, Agbarus, for believing in me, whom thou hast not seen: For it is written of me, that they which have seen me should not believe on me; that they which have not seen me may believe, and be saved. But concerning the Matter thou hast written about, these are to acquaint thee, That all things for which I am sent hither must be fulfilled, and then I shall be taken up and returned to him that sent me, but after my Ascension, I will send thee one of my Disciples, who shall cure thy Distemper, and give Life to thee, and to them that are with thee.

### Lentulus's *Epistle to the Senate of Rome, containing a Description of Jesus Christ.*

THERE appeared in these Days a Man of great Virtue called Jesus Christ, and by the People called a Prophet, but his own Disciples called him the Son of God. He raised the Dead, and cured all Manner of Diseases. A Man of Stature somewhat tall and comely, with a reverend Countenance, such as the Beholders may both fear and love. His Hair is the Colour of a Chestnut full ripe, and is plain down almost to his Ears, but from thence downwards it is something curled, but more orient of Colour, waving about his Shoulders. In the midst of his Head goeth down a Seam of Hair, or parting, like the Nazarites, his Forehead very plain and smooth, his Face without Spot or Wrinkle; beautiful with a comely red, his Nose and Mouth so formed, that nothing can be reprehended, his Beard thick the Colour of the Hair on his Head; his Eyes grey, clear and quick; in reproving he is severe, in counselling courteous; he is fair spoken, and pleasant in Speech, mixed with Gravity; it cannot be remembered that any have seen him laugh, but many have seen him weep; in Proportion of Body he is well shaped and straight; his Hands and Arms very delectable to behold; in speaking very temperate, modest and wise; a Man for singular Beauty far exceeding all the Sons of Men.

FINIS.

Printed and Sold by ADAMS & SONS, 5, 6, 7, East Street, Hereford.

In the days of open fires—at least until the 1960s, to my personal knowl-edge—midwives would burn the afterbirth. Some believed that the number of times it popped would denote the number of children the mother would subse-quently have. There was a strange notion in certain places that if a woman died in childbirth the clergyman could demand that the infant be christened over its mother's coffin.

It was customary for new babies to be given something silver, such as a sixpence: 'a tanner for the baby'. Some households put a bowl out for just such contributions from visitors after a birth. The first time a new baby is carried from the room in which it has been born it must be taken upstairs rather than down if it is to rise in the world. If no higher room existed someone would clamber on to a chair with the baby. Lest it grow up light-fingered the child would not have its nails cut, though they might be bitten short. There were different beliefs as to how long this should go on: only at the first trimming; until christening; for one year.

An early baptism was considered essential for a child's future well-being. An infant dying unbaptised would, according to an ancient belief, become a peewit—which might explain the bird's mournful cries. At the touch of the holy water at baptism it was lucky for the child to cry since this showed the depar-ture of an evil spirit. Particularly lusty crying predicted a good singer-to-be. Some churches would leave the north or devil's door open during the ceremony so that an evil spirit could depart from the building after quitting the child.

If children of different sexes were being baptised at the same ceremony girls had to precede boys. A woman who with seeming rudeness pushed past parents with boys so as to ensure that her baby girl was christened first offered this explanation:

> You see, sir, the parson bain't a married man, and consequentially is disfamiliar with children, or he'd a never put the little girl to be chris-tened after the boys. And though it sadly flustered me, sir, to put myself afore my betters in the way I was forced to do, yet, sir, it was a doing of a kindness to them two little boys, in me a setting of my girl afore 'em. Why? Well, sir, I har astonished as you don't know. Why, sir, if them little boys had been christened afore the little girl, they'd have had her soft chin, and she'd have had their hairy beards—the poor little innocent. But thank goodness I've kep' her from that misfortin'.

## Finding a husband

Both sexes must have been concerned about choosing a partner but women resorted to an extraordinary number of ways of trying to find out not only the identity of a future husband but how long they had to wait for him. A piece of wedding cake or a sprig of yarrow put under the pillow at night would induce a dream of one's husband-to-be. So—but no doubt rather uncomfortably—

would a breastbone, knife, fork and plate under the bolster; or a pair of new shoes and stockings worn through the night. A flowering branch of hawthorn could also be put under the pillow; or a woman could place her crossed shoes there (on a Friday) and recite:

> I put my left shoe over my right
> In hopes this night I may see
> The man that shall my husband be
> In his apparel and in his array
> And in the clothes he wears every day;
> What he does and what he wears
> And what he'll do all days and years,
> Whether I sleep or whether I wake
> I hope to hear my true love speak.

A letter from her love could be pinned in nine folds and put next to the heart before she went to bed. Then if she dreamed of gold and jewels he was sincere, otherwise not. Another test for sincerity was to take an apple pip, name the sweetheart, then put the pip on the fire. A bursting noise showed love; silent combustion meant its absence. Alternatively:

> If you love me bounce and fly;
> If you hate me lie and die.
> (or, If you're faithless, lie and die.)

Another test was to stick on the cheek as many pips as there were suitors, and to name them. The pip which fell off last would show the truest aspirant. A much more long-drawn process was to count up all the white horses seen until reaching the hundredth. After that the first man to whom the woman spoke—and this did give some room for manoeuvre—would be the one she married. At Eastnor it was believed that if an apple were pared, the unbroken peeling thrown over the left shoulder would fall in the shape of a future partner's first name.

The moon also featured in some rituals. A woman would go into the garden at the time of the first new moon of the year and say:

> New moon, new moon, tell unto me
> Which of these three is my husband to be.

Then she would name three men, curtseying each time. When next she saw them she had to notice whether they faced towards her or away. The one who happened to face her would be her husband. If they all faced she would probably have gone through the procedure a second time. Another appeal ran:

> New moon, new moon in the bright firmament,
> If [name] is my true love to be,
> Let the next time I see him
> His face be turned towards me.

A woman could also look through a silk handkerchief or a piece of frosted glass at the reflection of a new moon in a bucket of water. As many moons as she saw would be the number of months before she married. Timing could also be worked out by taking a ring and hanging it on a hair of one's own, then holding it over a glass of water. The number of times the ring knocked against the side of the glass would show the number of years before the wedding.

Further opportunities for divination arose on particular days during the course of the year. On St. Agnes' Eve (20 January) or All Hallow's Eve (31 October) women made and baked over the fire in complete silence a simple cake of flour, salt and water, called a Dumb Cake. If they then ate it or slept with it below the pillow they would dream of their future husband.

At midnight on Midsummer Eve (23 June) a young woman could go backwards into the garden, then move backwards round it, scattering hempseed with the right hand and intoning:

> Hempseed I sow;
> Hempseed is to mow;
> And the man that my husband is to be,
> Let him follow after and mow.

A vision of the future husband, scythe in hand, would then appear.

On the same day a woman could take two seedlings of the flowers called Orphine or Midsummer Men (*Sedum telephium*) and plant them in the house thatch, saying as she did so her own name and that of her sweetheart. If the flowers flourished a wedding would ensue; if not, the lovers would part. The same flowers were used for medicinal purposes. The Welsh herbal of the physicians of Myddfai recommended it against fever, sterility in women and over-profuse menstruation; in English cottage gardens it was grown as a 'gash herb' for immediate application to a wound.

At Hallowe'en women were advised:

> If you'd see the man you're to wed
> Touch with a lemon the posts of your bed.

They might also stand at midnight with lighted candle in front of a mirror, where the future husband's image would appear. One day later, at All Saints (1 November), a woman could sit at the window at midnight with a ball of new worsted thread. She took hold of one end of the yarn and threw out the ball with the words: 'Who holds?' The future husband would pick up the ball, say his name, then disappear.

On Christmas Eve three, five or seven women could meet for yet another ritual. Each took a sprig of rosemary—the herb of remembrance—and put it in a bowl of water in the centre of the room. A line stretched across held a white garment belonging to each. All sat in silence till midnight when the equivalent number of phantom men arrived, each taking a rosemary sprig and announcing his own name followed by that of his sweetheart.

On Christmas Day if a woman wore a rose plucked the previous Midsummer Eve a single man who took it would marry her. Objects put in Christmas puddings were also employed for divination. A portion found to contain a silver ring showed the recipient would marry within the year; a bone button—known as the bachelor's button—carried the message that the finder would remain single.

A Dumb Cake, as mentioned above, was also made on New Year's Eve and eaten by a group of women. One of them next put on a chemise—the use of the term indicates the period when the practice was current—on a chair in front of the fire, inside out, and sprinkled it with water from a sprig of rosemary. A silent vigil was maintained until midnight, when the form of the husband of any of the women to be married in the ensuing year would appear by the fire and turn the chemise.

By contrast with such acute anxiety about a future husband the approach of men to their choice of partner was laconic and down to earth: 'Boy, you take a good look round the meadow before you find the gate'. Such good sense was echoed by at least one woman, who said 'There's more to marriage than four bare legs in a bed'.

Whereas cradles—and also grandfather clocks—were passed down the male side of families, Welsh dressers and dower chests firmly belonged to the female line. The chests, often centuries old, were used to accumulate household linen long before a woman had chosen a partner. Once she had done so collecting for the chest or bottom drawer went on apace.

## Marriage

The reading of banns in churches attracted different beliefs in different places. Some thought it unlucky for either party to hear all three readings; some for the couple to hear any readings together; some for the woman to hear any. Similarly, certain days—Wednesday or Friday, for example—were considered unlucky by some for weddings. For marriage, as for birth, the month of May was thought unlucky: 'Marry in May, repent for aye'. Some also avoided the whole of Lent and also the week of Easter.

The old notion that the bride should wear something old, something new, something borrowed, something blue, is still widely held—or at least the prac-

*A wedding at Little Cowarne in the 1950s, with the arch over the gate decorated with flowers*

tice is followed. The bride should not see her reflection in the mirror on her wedding morning once she is fully dressed for the ceremony; nor should she turn back on any account once she has set off from home for the church. It is also unlucky for the bride and groom to leave by a back door after their reception. That they should not see each other on their wedding day until they meet in church is also widely accepted, even by couples who have been living together for some years before deciding to marry.

Some weddings used to be timed to begin at five minutes past the hour so that the clock should not strike during the service, thus avoiding another bad omen. Ringers might predict the number of children to be born to a couple by the number of strokes of the great bell after the final peal for the wedding.

*A wedding at Peterstow, c.1900*

At Peterchurch a groom who omitted to pay the ringers was censured by their ringing the bells backwards as a kind of curse. It was a very bad sign if a ringer overthrew a bell when ringing a wedding peal or if a bellrope broke.

Mothers made sure that a bride always carried in her bouquet some myrtle, an emblem of peace, love and happiness. One song says:

> In the middle of the ocean there shall grow a myrtle tree
> Before I ever prove false to her, the girl that loves me.

A groom at Cusop was greeted by a different plant as he emerged from church with his bride on his arm. A woman he had jilted threw a handful of rue at him, with the words 'May you rue this day as long as you live'.

The better-disposed threw things with happier associations. Kilvert noted in 1874 of the wedding of his friend, Rev. Andrew Pope, to Miss Money Kyrle that in the churchyard at Much Marcle 'the bride's path was strewn with flowers'. At a similar ceremony in the same year, 'Our dear little bride', he wrote, 'went off with her husband happy and radiant amid blinding showers of rice and old shoes'. Rice stood for plenty, and the old shoes symbolised the transfer of authority over the woman from the father to the husband. The latter notion at least would be indignantly rejected by today's brides, and the shoes tied to honeymoon cars are just an expression of good luck wishes.

Couples are often met at the church door by a guard of honour. For huntsmen a pack of hounds is sometimes whipped in. At Dorstone salutes to newly-weds were once fired on the blacksmith's anvil. Gunpowder charges in a hole in the base were set off by a fuse, causing the anvil to jump and a loud report to be heard. In the same village maroons which normally warned of fog were placed on the railway lines and fired by trains taking couples on honeymoon.

*Roping the bride at Eardisland in the 1950s*

As late as the mid-1990s some villagers at Eardisland remembered a former custom of children tying a rope across the road leading from the church after a wedding. Once the bride and groom had paid a small fee they were allowed to continue through, having passed another small landmark at the beginning of their new life together.

Before Lord Hardwicke's Marriage Act came into force in 1754—it was this which made the reading of banns a legal requirement—couples could be married 'by consent', with few formalities. Long afterwards, ordinary people believed in the legality of a summary form of divorce and re-marriage. First a husband had to 'sell' his wife. A 90-year-old woman who wrote to the *Hereford Times* in April and May 1876 had personal knowledge of a number of cases. 'I have seen several wives bought and sold in the market', she claimed. 'One man who bought ... lived in Price's Hospital, and that was the woman who carried the bloody loaf in the bread riots [of 1800]'. Far from acquiring a compliant partner, the man, perhaps unknown to him, was linking up with a brave character whose part, with others, in direct action to bring down the price of a staple commodity, inspired a local song:

> Have you not heard of our Herefordshire women?
> How they ran and left their spinning,
> How they ran without hat or feather
> To fight for bread, 'twas through all weather.
> Oh, our brave Herefordshire women!

'Nonagenarian' went on to describe in detail another wife sale in Hereford:

I must recall to your memory my statement as to my being playfellow to Mona Delnotte Coates, for it was while walking out with her and her attendant that I first saw a man selling his wife. We were going from the Barton to the other side of the town, and necessarily had to pass the bottom of the pig market. Here we saw a crowd. The girl was desirous of knowing what was the matter, so she elbowed her way through the people, and was followed by the children to the open space in the centre. There stood a woman with her hat in her hand. All classes of women wore hats very much like those worn now, only as artificial flowers were then very dear, they were covered all over the tops with massive bows, and sometimes had a plume of feathers. The woman's hat was a very smart one. She stood looking down. At first I thought she was admiring her own red cloak, but as she stood so still my eye wandered over to see what was amiss; and I shall never forget how surprised I felt when I observed she had a rope about her neck, and that a man was holding one end of it. 'What has she done?' we both cried out, for I believed she was going to be hanged. 'Oh', said a bystander, 'she has done no good, depend upon it, or else he wouldn't want to sell her'. Just then there was a loud laugh and a man shouted: 'Well done, Jack, that is eleven pence more than I would give; it's too much, boy, too much'. But Jack stood firm. 'No', said he. 'I'll give a shilling, no more, and he ought to be thankful to be rid of her at any price'. 'Well', said the man, 'I'll take it, though her looks ought to bring more than that'. 'Keep her, master, keep her for her good looks', shouted the laughing bystanders. 'No', said he. 'good looks won't put the victuals on the table for me without willing hands'. 'Well', said Jack, 'here's the shilling, and I warn't I'll make her put the victuals on the table for me, and help to get it first; be you willing, missis, to leave him and take me for better or worse?' 'I be willing', said she. 'And be you willing to sell her for what I bid, master?' 'I be', said he, 'and will give you the rope into the bargain'. So Jack gave the man his shilling, and the man put the rope into Jack's hand, and Jack walked off up the pig market leading his newly bought wife by the halter.

The writer knew the couple subsequently, and reported that the woman was 'a bit of a mag [scold] but he conquered her', and that she worked hard to help him in his trade of weaving. They had one son.

'Nonagenarian' went on to mention another woman sold in a similar fashion, this time in the butter market, and then in contradiction of the view that such events invariably involved consenting parties observed: 'Several years

*Fanciful illustration of a wife sale*

afterwards a much more dreadful sale took place in Hereford for the individuals were very unwilling to be sold, and upon their bended knees bitterly cried and entreated not to be sold'. One wonders whether the reference here includes the wife sold in Hereford in 1802 by a butcher for £1 4s. and a bowl of punch.

A further case was reported from Leominster in 1818. Another, even later, was described by Andrew Haggard in 1972:

> J.R. when in his late seventies, about 1930, told me that his mother had seen a man sell his wife in Bromyard market for a few shillings. ... According to J.R., the woman in only her shift was led into the market on a halter like an animal. Asking why a man should accept such a small sum, I was told that if he gave her away she could come back, but if sold even for a shilling she could not. J.R. concluded: 'I expect he wur well shut on her'.

The wearing of the shift, which also occurred even in some church weddings, arose from the belief that this exempted a woman's future husband from liability from any debts she might have incurred previously.

A sanction imposed on women was the 'scold's bridle', of which an example is preserved in Hereford Museum. This iron gag with supporting framework would have been clamped round the head of an allegedly turbulent woman for so many hours. More serious was the gum- or ducking-stool which magistrates could order not only for sharp-tongued women but for short-weighing or otherwise cheating tradesmen. Until the sixteenth century the Bromyard grimstool or gumstool was kept in Church Lane when not in use.

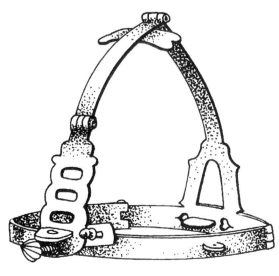

*A Scold's Bridle*

The Leominster stool, a formidable structure originally used in Worcester, has survived and is kept in the Priory Church. The device, widely used from the fifteenth to the seventeenth centuries, is frequently mentioned in the town records, often as being in need of repair. The last ducking in Leominster—and probably in England—took place in 1809, when Jenny Pipes was paraded before being lowered into the Lugg. The stool was wheeled out again with Sarah Leake in

*Leominster's ducking stool (above) and an example of 'rough music' (below)*

1817 but she escaped ducking because the river was too low. Jenny Pipes now lends her name to a local beer.

A sign of communal rather than judicial disapproval involved parading originally people and later effigies astride poles, to the accompaniment of rough music—beating pans, kettles or shovels, blowing whistles or cow horns, waving rattles and bawling comments. There is a record that as early as 1587 William Pilinger was carried on a 'colestaffe' at Cradley for some offence. Several men were called to account at Hereford consistory court not so much for the colestaffing itself, but because it was done 'in the tyme of divyne service, with the blowing of hornes, and throwing of graynes [grains], with such other fantasticall toyes'. Several centuries later, Mrs. Leather wrote:

> A figure made of straw is placed astride a long pole and is carried to the house of the offender [such as an unfaithful husband or wife] it is meant to represent, accompanied by a crowd with pots, pans, and tins, making as much noise as possible. Near the house a large bonfire is made, in which the effigy is burnt. This was done at Leominster and at Weobley

Marsh within the last twenty years [that is, between 1892 and 1912] . I was told by an old man at Llanveyno that he had seen it done a few years since at Walterstone; he could not remember the date.

An account by a Charles Stephens of a similar episode in his native Kington, 'about 65 years ago', appeared in the volume of the Woolhope Society's *Transactions* published in 1952:

> The victim was a woman of the name of Price who practised midwifery. What the scandal was about I do not know, but I well remember our char-woman taking me to see the sight. It was a dark, wet November night. A procession was formed and led by a man named Halters, or Slaters, and known locally as 'Roper'. He carried the effigy, on which was a placard bearing the words:
>
> > Too wet to burn her,
> > Too dark to hang her,
> > So we must let her go afloat.
>
> A mob followed beating trays, pans, etc., and eventually arrived at the cottage which was facing the river Arrow, then high in flood. After a noisy demonstration the doggerel was proclaimed and the effigy thrown over the wall into the river. This was the last Stang riding practised in Kington.

## Death

A host of signs were thought to give warning of imminent death, and many of these are given in chapter 5. Parishioners at Bredwardine thought that Kilvert's death in 1879 was foreshadowed by an omen, that of a bell at the church which rang with a 'heavy sound'. Families would interpret as other harbingers events such as the fall of an old tree.

Those wishing for precise prediction could take ivy leaves, write on them the names of members of their family, and steep them in water overnight at Hallowe'en. Next morning the leaves corresponding with those members of the family who were to die during the ensuing year would bear the mark of a coffin. Some thought that if one listened on the same night at the door of the church the devil would be heard reading inside a list of the names of those due to die within twelve months. At Kington, close to the Welsh border, people once believed in the corpse candle, a ghostly light seen leaving a house where a death would occur, then moving to the churchyard and hovering where the grave would be dug.

The passing of a person close to death would be assisted by removing the pillow from beneath the head. All doors would be unlocked and opened so that the soul's departure would not be hindered.

Bees had to be told of family events such as births, marriages and deaths. It was widely believed that if the ceremony were omitted the bees would either die or leave. The hive would sometimes be dressed with black crepe, and turned round as the corpse left the house.

The sins of the departed could be assumed by a kind of scapegoat, the sin eater. John Aubrey—who owned estates in Herefordshire at Burleton and Stretford—wrote the classic account of this practice in the seventeenth century:

> In the County of Hereford was an old Custome at Funeralls to hire poor people, who were to take upon them all the Sinnes of the party deceased. One of them I remember (he was a long leane, lamentable poor raskal) lived in a cottage on Rosse-high-way. The manner was that when the Corps was brought-out of the house and layd on the Biere; a Loafe of bread was brought out, and delivered to the Sinne-eater over the corps, as also a Mazar-bowle [of Maple] full of beer, which he was to drinke up, and sixpence in money, in consideration whereof he tooke upon him (*ipso facto*) all the Sinnes of the Defunct, and freed him [or her] from Walking after they were dead. ...
>
> This Custome (though rarely used in our dayes) yet by some people was observed even in the strictest time of the Presbyterian government [the Commonwealth]: as at Dynder [Dinedor], *volens nolens* [willy nilly] the Parson of the Parish, the kindred of a woman deceased there, had this ceremonie punctually performed, according to her Will. And also the like was donne at the City of Hereford in those times, where a Woman kept many years before her death a Mazard-bowle for the Sinne-eater: and the like in other places in this Countie.

According to local tradition, Aubrey's sin-eater lived in a poor cottage close to the present Traveller's Rest Inn, by the roundabout at the western end of the M50. However, another sin-eater features in a seventeenth-century story of star-crossed lovers in Ross. A young gardener, Roger Mortimer, who worked at Alton Court half a mile south-east of the town, fell in love with his employer's second daughter, the beautiful Clara Markey. She reciprocated, but they were fully aware of the social gulf between them and therefore kept their feelings secret. To their dismay the time came when Clara's father told her that he had arranged for her to marry a young man from the well-to-do Rudhall family. (Monuments to both Markeys and Rudhalls can still be seen in Ross Church).

Mortimer was so distraught that an old woman called Nancy Carter was accused of bewitching him. Straws in the shape of a cross were strewn after her and pins plunged into her in attempts to lift the imagined spell. (Drawing a witch's blood was thought to remove her powers). Then Mortimer's hat was discovered lodged against the central pier of Wilton Bridge, and searchers found his body upstream, near The Acres. The body was carried to the Welsh Harp Inn, Alton Street, and Jack 'the Scape' Clements who lived in Walford Road was hired as sin eater. A quart of beer and sixpence were passed over the

*Wilton Bridge, where Mortimer's hat was found lodged
against the central pier*

corpse to him, and he stated: 'I takes all the consequences and so I has all the beer'.

After sunset the body was taken up the road and buried without ceremony other than the driving of a stake through the heart, so as 'to be sure he would not walk, and bite people in their beds'. That was how Corpse Cross (now Copse Cross) acquired its name, though Mrs. Leather suggests it is a corruption of Corpus Christi Cross. (The bodies of those who had committed suicide were buried there in similar fashion until 1823, when the law ended the practice).

Clara's marriage was due only a few days after the burial. In Ross Church when the parson enquired whether she would take Rudhall as a husband she uttered a scream, then fainted. She was taken home unconscious, but half an hour later she was found wandering in a daze, seeking where Mortimer had been buried at the crossroads on Alton Road. Her family led her home, but every time she could escape their vigilance she would slip away to pace slowly up and down the lane leading to Corpse Cross. Eventually she was given her head, and made her lonely walk for decades until she herself died. The lane is still called Old Maid's Walk.

In the twentieth century Mary Webb inserted a fictional sin-eating passage into her novel *Precious Bane* (1924) set in Shropshire. There is no evidence from that period in Shropshire, but Mrs. Leather mentions a Herefordshire relic of the custom in the drinking of port wine and the eating of biscuits at Craswall and Walterstone in the room where a body lies. In 1926 the bishop of Hereford, Dr. Linton Smith, reported being told by a woman from the north of the county that when her child died 'the nurse pressed her to lay a piece of bread on the breast of the dead body'. He considered this to be another survival of 'sin-bread'. Perhaps another trace of the custom was the practice at Eastnor of putting salt on the eyes of a corpse to keep them closed.

Before a funeral procession left the house it was customary for the deceased's will to be read or to be passed over the coffin to the legatee. Some country solicitors still follow this procedure.

Coffins were sometimes carried long distances by relays of bearers, and it was not done to refuse a request to act as a bearer. Whether the route were long or short householders kept their curtains drawn along it until the coffin had passed. This was either a mark of respect or because it was unlucky to see a funeral procession through glass, or a combination of the two. When a coffin had to be carried from an isolated house across cultivated fields it was believed that a right of way would be created unless some payment, if only a few pence, were exacted by the landowner. Alternatively, a detour could be made to avoid private ground.

*Wooden effigy of Sir Walter de Helyon at Much Marcle Church*

At Ross mourners sang psalms before the corpse on its journey from house to church. In former times an effigy of the deceased was carried before the coffin, and this practice was followed at Much Marcle until 1878. One effigy, that of the fourteenth-century franklin, Sir Walter de Helyon, is still kept in the church there. Another, that of a priest dating from about 1300, is at Clifford; it resembles in turn the effigy of Bishop Aquablanca (died 1268) at Hereford Cathedral.

Richard Parry, the nineteenth-century historian of Kington, wrote that 'When a funeral procession arrived at a cross road, it was the custom ... to put down the corpse for a few moments, and for the mourners and others to stand still'. At Brilley the coffin was carried three times round the Funeral Stone (which has now gone) by the churchyard gate before passing through. The manoeuvre was thought to ensure that the devil could not take the soul of the deceased. The same notion probably lay behind the Pembridge custom of taking a round-about route with the coffin, then going right round the churchyard 'the way of the sun'.

At Ocle Pychard and elsewhere in North Herefordshire all the church bells are chimed when the funeral procession approaches. This is called 'ringing home' or 'welcoming home' the deceased.

If at all possible bearers would avoid entering church or churchyard on the north side. At Leysters, for

*Engraving of a funeral from a ballad sheet—see page 166*
*(based on the reversed image of an original woodcut by Thomas Bewick)*

example, funerals always entered the churchyard by the east gate and paused at a funeral stone from which the cortege would be read into the church by the vicar. The north or devil's side was reserved for suicides and strangers, and unacceptable for burials. Since the usual door for access was on the south side the dead buried there would receive the prayers of the living as they passed the graves and read the inscriptions. People were buried on an east-west alignment, looking towards the east from whence the resurrection would come.

Orleton in Herefordshire was for some reason thought to be the place where the resurrection would begin on the Day of Judgement. People from all over England arranged to be buried there, thinking they would be the first to rise from their graves.

By a cruel irony the name of resurrectionists was given to those who stole newly-buried bodies for dissection. In 1832 at Hereford two men were arrested for stealing the body of an army veteran, William Hardman—it was found in a hamper opened at the local coach-office. The men appeared before the mayor, and as they were on their way to gaol 'they were followed by an immense crowd, and assailed with the most vociferous expressions of disgust and contempt'. Long after the Anatomy Act of 1832 legalised and regularised the supply of corpses for dissection, stories continued to be told of the hated resurrection men. Soon after the burial of Emma Foulger in 1855 at Aylton (see also page 126) her grave was found open and the body missing.

In the Golden Valley a premature rising in the form of a ghost was averted when the need was felt by burying a corpse face down. Shakespeare's 'rosemary for remembrance' is still planted on graves as a token that the dead are not forgotten.

Two stories from Eastnor show a passionate posthumous devotion to the place. A woman from the village dying of fever in the West Indies expressed a fervent wish to be buried in 'the old churchyard'. Her husband, unable to obtain the necessary permission to ship her body to England, put it into a cask of rum and smuggled it to Eastnor for burial, thus fulfilling his wife's last request.

Another woman who hailed from elsewhere but had spent much of her life in the parish also wanted to be buried there. Her husband demurred, possibly because he preferred their native place, but acquiesced when she threatened to haunt him:

*Emma Foulger's grave at Aylton*

If you do bury mer in --- [the other] churchyard I'll tell you what I'll do. When you be coming hoam by the church path from the Pig and Whistle o' Saturday nights, a full o' cider, I'll stand up in front o' yer, and yer'll hev to get by mer.

# CHAPTER 5

# Superstitions

When life is precarious superstitions abound. Even in today's relatively secure society few people will claim to be completely without some little taboo or odd belief. Few of such superstitions are peculiar to particular places and many have national and even international currency. An exception which may prove the rule is apparently specific to the village of Mathon, where there is a belief that if part of a particular field is inadvertently left unsown a death in the farmer's family will follow within a year.

Explanation for superstitions is often hard to find. The word literally means 'standing over something in awe or amazement', and it has overtones of mystery and fear. Touching wood to avert ill-luck may date back to the practice of touching a fragment thought to come from Christ's cross. Alternatively, pre-Christian religions venerated trees so the superstition may go back to very early times. Whatever the truth of this may be, the feeling that possible misfortune needs to be warded off can easily well up. In August 1991 chain letters from Venezuela started to arrive in Ledbury. They promised good fortune if the recipients sent copies to 20 people within four days, death and disaster otherwise. Those who complied would receive sums of money out of the blue, or offers of jobs. One man who broke the chain—so it was alleged—died nine days later; another lost his wife. Police advised people to tear up the letters, and offered to do so themselves for anyone too frightened to follow their advice. This was far from being the last instance of such events.

Folk medicine, especially the herbal variety, seems to be enjoying a new lease of life, though some of the wilder remedies for such things as whooping cough are unlikely to return. Nevertheless, within living memory a charm was used at Dorstone to ensure that when a tree was cut down it fell in the right place.

Weather lore is facing stiff competition from scientific meteorology but still has much to offer, even though global warming is beginning to undermine tested sayings such as (in January) 'when the days lengthen the cold strengthens'. A great deal of wisdom and humour is encapsulated in traditional rhymes and sayings. One writer dismissed all superstitions as 'fooleries' but many would reject such a peremptory judgement.

## Sayings

Practical wisdom found expression in a host of semi-proverbial axioms such as: 'an ounce of help is worth a wagon load of pity'; 'a good contriver is better than an early riser'; 'dilly-dally brings night as soon as hurry-scurry'; 'and I was born too near a 'ood (wood) to be frightened by owls'. There is wry humour in such comments as 'a good man round a barrel but no cooper' and (applied to a woman with a boorish husband) 'Her'll never want for bacon; her's allus got a hog in the house'. In the same vein are 'The wind be that lazy it fair goes through yer' and 'I be that 'ungry me stomach thinks me throat be cut'.

Set comparisons were much appreciated. 'As busy as an ant' can still be heard, together with 'as fat (or slick, or smooth) as an oont' (mole), 'as sour as varges' (crab vinegar) and 'as useless as a sundial in a cellar'. A child grows 'like a hop-vine' and a grating voice is 'like a humble bee in a churn'. 'As long as the oak and ash grow' means for ever.

## Signs

A large number of omens forewarned of possible misfortune. In the 1990s some nurses at Bosbury told me that a series of creases making the shape of a coffin in a newly laundered sheet were a sign of death. A similar portent was created if a person brought the first snowdrops of the season into the house, opened an umbrella there, shouldered a spade or dropped scissors so that they fell on one point. (To fall on the two together indicated a wedding).

Other tell-tale objects presaging misfortune were a clock falling, a church bell being rung as the clock strikes, a winding sheet—that is, an unburnt wavelet of wax curling away from the flame—on a candle, or a wick glowing long after it is extinguished, or a long run in black suits during a game of cards. Signs of death indicated by plants included the blooming of an apple tree twice a year or its bearing fruit and blossom at the same time, the dying off or shrivelling of a gooseberry or currant bush while it is fruiting, the death of ivy on a house, and the appearance of a rose with leaves between the petals. Certain animal behaviour was seen in a similar light—the howling of a dog, the coughing of a cat, rats' nibbling furniture, the entry to a house of a mole, frog or toad, the flight of a white bird against a window or the tapping of any bird at a pane.

The actions of birds were carefully watched. The flight of a bird over a sickbed signalled the death of its occupant. A robin's entering a house gave the same warning, though a bee's incursion meant a visit from a stranger. (So did a cock crowing in an open doorway, or a lid accidentally left off the teapot). Otherwise the robin was a lucky bird. As was the wren:

> Malisons, malisons, more than ten,
> Who kills the Queen of Heaven's wren.

It was considered unlucky to destroy a swallow's nest or kill an owl. The latter was favoured because it flew out of the oak tree not when Charles II hid in it but when searchers arrived, thus causing them to miss the fugitive. To see a raven was a bad sign. Magpies varied:

> One for sorrow, two for mirth;
> Three for a wedding, four for a birth.

An Eastnor variant on this rhyme continued:

> Five's a christening, six is a dearth,
> Seven is heaven, eight is hell,
> Nine's the devil his very sel'.

Two crows meant a wedding, and one a funeral. The Seven Whistlers passing overhead at night portended disaster. There is uncertainty as to what these birds were, and this perhaps increases the fear. One possibility is the swift, known in Herefordshire as 'the devil screamer'.

Despite its unpleasant habits the cuckoo does not bring ill luck. Some believed, though, that whatever one was doing on first hearing it would be one's main occupation through the ensuing year. Rain is predicted by the call of the stormcock (another name for the green woodpecker or yaffle), the bray of the donkey and the closing during daylight of the scarlet pimpernel.

A very long list of actions or omissions brings bad luck or unpleasant consequences. Kicking fungi leads to seven years' bad luck. The results of picking herb robert (*Geranium robertarium*) are shown in its local name Death-come-quickly. Ill luck comes of taking into the house snowdrops before 1 May, or mistletoe or holly before Christmas. Elder wood should not be burnt at all, and no wood should be burnt green—'Burn green, sorrow soon seen'—except for pear: 'Pear dry, pear green, makes a fire fit for a queen'. Red and white flowers in the same bunch are considered unlucky, especially in hospitals, where they may point to blood on the sheets. Parsley should not be transplanted: 'Well, if you plants parsley you plants the Old Man'. The willow is cursed since the Virgin Mary whipped her son with it and caused him to say, in the words of *The Bitter Withy* (see also chapter 8):

> Cursed be the sally tree which maketh me to smart;
> The sally tree shall be the first to perish at the heart.

How cricketers escape from this injunction is not clear, but there was a time when no countryman would hit an animal with a stick of willow.

A hare running down a village street showed that there would be a fire. A weasel crossing one's path was unlucky; so was the first lamb or colt of the season if it were seen facing away. Killing a ladybird was also unlucky, and so with many other things which people carelessly did or left undone.

Salt was a precious commodity, and also a symbol for immortality. Formerly, when moving from a house people left some bread and salt, or ill-luck would come to both leavers and the in-comers. Spilling salt was decidedly unlucky: in Leonardo da Vinci's painting of the Last Supper Judas is shown overturning the salt, but the superstition may pre-date the picture. Returning borrowed salt was unlucky; so was putting salt on someone else's food, rather than simply passing it. Still at table, crossing knives led to a quarrel, but this could be averted if the lower of the two were withdrawn, and these words said: 'Blessed are the peacemakers'. Putting new shoes on the table is still considered unlucky by many.

A quarrel can again be caused when two people wash in the same water, unless the second spits in it first. Giving knives or scissors as a present leads to the end of a friendship unless something is given in exchange. However, the gift of a pin should not be repaid, even with thanks. A light should not be given at Christmas or the New Year, and being one of a party of thirteen was especially unlucky at Christmas.

Throwing out soapsuds on Holy Thursday (the Thursday before Easter) was unlucky, and hanging out clothes to dry on the same day would ensure that there would be a death in the family, with the corpse laid out in one of the items on the line. Good Friday was thought to be a special day for planting since this was 'the only day the devil has no right to the ground'. However, to leave soapsuds in a boiler over Good Friday will lead to a death in the house, and washing on the day brings bad luck for twelve months. At Weobley there was a belief that nothing should be poured down the sink until after 3 p.m. on Good Friday since the gutters of Jerusalem were running with Christ's blood till that time.

The phases of the moon were carefully watched, since planting had to be done as it waxed, and also the killing of animals and even the cutting of hair:

> Crop your head in the moon's wax,
> Ne'er cut it in the wane;
> And then of a bald head
> You shall never complain.

Pointing at a new moon (and also a rainbow) is unlucky; so is to see it first through glass. When it is seen in the open people should turn the money in their pockets and wish for a lucky month.

Certain days were unlucky, especially Friday—the day of the crucifixion—when fresh work should not be undertaken nor a journey begun nor a mattress turned. Cutting nails on a Sunday—a Friday in some versions—was to be avoided:

> Better had he never been born
> Than pare his nails on a Sunday morn.

Further ill luck came from saying goodbye over a stile or at a crossroads; shaking hands over a gate or hedge; treading on a piece of iron; meeting or passing someone on the stairs; going back over the doorstep for something forgotten (unless a person sits down and counts to ten to break the spell); passing beneath a ladder (unless bad luck is averted by crossing the fingers and thumbs); and even meeting a squinting woman (unless one speaks to her). When a fire was lit the devil was shamed when logs were crossed, and a useful tip was:

> One log can't burn.
> Two logs won't burn.
> Three logs make a fire.

If a chimney failed to draw, a cross was made by placing a poker against the bars of the fire to drive the devil out.

Very few things seemed to bring good luck. A black cat crossing one's path is still very well known, but a fox's doing so at night is also lucky. Some farmers thought white cows lucky; others, a flock of sheep or a load of hay encountered on a journey. Certain omens were inescapable. A burning face indicates that someone is talking about the person. A shudder shows that someone is walking over the spot where one's grave is to be. An itchy foot will soon be treading strange ground; an itching ear portends news from the living; a nose, bad news or that 'You will be kissed, cursed or vexed, or shake hands with a fool'. When rosemary flourishes in a garden, the mistress is master. So too if the lavender does well, or the sage thrives.

## Charms

Horseshoes nailed to doors or fixed over bedsteads performed the double function of keeping away witches and bringing good luck. Some favoured the points up, others down. The former is associated with the horned moon, the latter with the Greek omega.

Rowan—otherwise known as witty, wittan or wittern—also provided protection against witches, both as a living tree and as detached pieces. Of the time when he was a boy in the 1630s, John Aubrey wrote that Herefordshire

*Roman altar at Michaelchurch*

people 'made the pinnes for the yoakes of their oxen' from the 'whitty-tree', 'believing it had the vertue to preserve them from being fore-spoken, as they call it; and they used to plant one by their dwelling-house, believing it to preserve them from witches and evill eyes'. Parson Kilvert found Hannah Preece's cottage on Monnington Common hung with rowan and birch twigs which served 'to keep the old witch out' and were renewed annually on May Eve.

Many villages once had a healer or charmer. The top of the Roman altar now in the church at Michaelchurch near Ross, once kept in a cottage which stood on the edge of the churchyard near the gate, was used (noted Rev. W.D. Barber) 'by a village doctress to pound herbs in'. Weobley was noted for its herbalists and charmers.

Mrs. Leather obtained a manuscript dated 1804 in which John E. of Weobley recorded charms against toothache, burns, ague, sprains, cuts, the bite of a mad dog, thorn wounds and spells. Elizabeth Hughes (1755-1849), 'the Kingsland doctress', became very widely known. The loss of one of her twin children in 1802 led to a great spiritual crisis, after which she became convinced that 'she might perform miracles in the cure of lameness, blindness and all morbid affections'. She proceded to lay hands on those who consulted her, and the cures she achieved brought patients from as far afield as Portsmouth and Northallerton. Some thought Hughes a fraud, and when she died the Kingsland rector, R.D. Evans, recorded: 'Formerly a celebrated Charmer. Persons came from all parts to be cured of their diseases; about 45 years ago. A great imposter'. On the other hand, an unsigned letter (possibly by the quaker, John Southall) to the *Hereford Times*, described her as 'a respectable, matronly-looking countrywoman' and concluded: 'That she was no mere mercenary or wilful imposter is, to my mind, satisfactorily proved by the circumstances of her having rejected the pecuniary gifts of her patients'.

During her childhood at Eastnor a Mrs. Guise, daughter of Rev. Pulling, who was incumbent there from 1847-94, remembered 'wise' people who 'performed feats of witchcraft with incantations'. As a young adult she recalled 'a boy being sent to an old wizard to be tanged, that is touched, for nose-bleeding'.

*Dorstone in the 1930s (from a postcard)*

As recently as the 1930s Lizzie Watkins of Dorstone was both feared and respected as a folk doctor and herbalist. Amongst her charms were those for toothache and warts, muttering words which have not been recorded, and were probably not meant to be. Other charms have been documented elsewhere:

### Burns

There were two angels came from the north.
One brought frost and the other brought fire.
In, frost. Out, fire.
In the name of the Father, Son and Holy Ghost. (Mathon)

### Cuts

A Charm for Stopping Blood: Our blessed Lord and Saviour was baptised in the River Jordan; the waters was wild, the Child was mild the water was blest and still it stood sweet Jesus Christ in Charity stop this blood. (Weobley)

### Toothache

The following was written on a small piece of paper and sealed with pitch:

Christ met with Peter and saide unto him Peter what is the mater with the. Peter saide lorde I am tormented with the pains in the tooth the worme shall die and Thou shalt live and thow that shalt have this in wrightin or in memory shall never have the Paine in the tooth. Therefore believe in the lorde youre God. (Craswall, 1886)

The notion that such charms could have therapeutic powers seems ludicrous but apparently they often worked on the principle, no doubt, of faith healing. They embody a curious mixture of magical practice and religious faith, and must at times have been last ditch attempts at finding a cure when proper medical treatment was wanting.

## Desperate Remedies

Certain substances were thought to have particular powers. Iron retained from primitive times a reputation for efficacity against witchcraft. The gold of a wedding ring blessed during the marriage ceremony could cure certain ailments (see below). Lead stolen from a church roof was doubly effective—for many years a cross made of lead taken from Cusop Church hung in the neighbouring Blackhill Farm, where it was thought to give protection against fire and lightning. Water left over in a font after a baptism was eagerly sought for its curative properties. Rev. A.H. Sayce noted in 1923 that one day he had asked his colleague, Rev. Morgan-Watkins, vicar of Kentchurch 'whether the peasantry in his district still regarded the consecrated water of the font as a sure and certain specific for sore eyes, epileptic fits and the like'. His reply was:

> Certainly, and I let them have as much of its as they wish; but I draw the line at the Communion Alms. ... The money of the offertory in the Communion Service; they are constantly bringing me sixpences and shillings which they want me to exchange for the offertory silver, and the latter is considered a more sovereign remedy than even the holy water of the font when put under the pillow at night or put into the pocket by day.

The ceremony of baptism itself was considered a helpful step for a weakly or fractious infant, and consecrated wine was regarded as a useful medicine. Personal amulets were widely carried. A double hazel nut or a potato in the pocket could ward off ill luck. A bloodstone gave protection against bleeding. The touch of some people, from dead man to living monarch, could also have therapeutic effects.

The principles involved in folk medicine range from faith healing to the use of substances now known to be chemically beneficial, such as cobwebs to staunch bleeding. They include would-be magical transference of disease to other people, animals, or objects. Some of the remedies, though, could have exacerbated rather than allayed disease. For example, a suggested cure for rabies caused by a mad dog was to write a few words on a piece of cheese and give it to the animal to eat.

## Ague

Go to a tree grafter. Tell him what is the matter and then go away. When you are at home he will cut the first branch of a maiden ash and you will be cured. (The same technique was used for rupture).

## Baldness

Wear a cowpat on the head in bed. Wear a cap made of ivy leaves.

## Cholera

Eat grated crumbs from bread baked on a Good Friday and kept till the following Good Friday. At Bredwardine, Much Marcle and elsewhere, small loaves of two to three inches in diameter were cooked on Good Friday to be saved, then ground to powder and mixed with hot water to be given for a variety of common ailments.

## Cramp

Wear an eelskin garter below the knee. Wear a ring made from a coffin hinge or a consecrated shilling. There is a record of a mid-seventeenth-century goldsmith in Hereford who was brought such coins 'by Papists' to have cramp rings made. Alternatively, be christened or confirmed, as appropriate (also a cure for fits).

## Dog bite

Pluck three hairs from the dog's tail and swallow them.

## Fits

Drink an infusion made from mistletoe growing on hawthorn. Wear on the finger or on string round the neck a ring made from sacrament silver—a coin given in collection at church, and blessed by clergymen. Parsons were frequently asked for 'sacrament shillings' for this purpose, and the remedy was widely employed.

## Jaundice

Take the inner rind of elder bark boiled in milk.

## Nose Bleed

Put church key on string down inside the sufferer's shirt or dress (Thruxton).

## Rheumatism

Carry a piece of alder wood in a pocket. Lay a hop pillow under the bed. (The latter remedy was prescribed for George III by a doctor at Reading).

### Rupture
Slit a sapling; walk between the halves, then tie them up. The ash was chosen at Broxwood, Thruxton and Walterstone; the willow at Eardisland.

### Scrofula
Be touched by a king.

### Shingles
Apply grease from the bearings of a church bell.

### Sore eyes
Apply water from a holy well, or rainwater caught
and bottled on Ascension Day.

### Sore feet
Put silverweed (*Potentilla anserina*, locally known as Traveller's Ease)
in the shoes.

### Stitch after running
Fix crosses to shoes.

### Stye
Rub with wedding ring.

### Teething
Hang bag of woodlice round baby's neck.

### Toothache
Wear oont's (mole's) feet in bag round neck; or, also round the neck, a spider in a nutshell. Carry the gall of a wild rose.

### Viper bite
Wrap affected part in a skin taken warm and reeking from a sheep. Or kill the snake, then make a paste of its liver and eat it. Adder skins were used to cure wounds made by thorns.

### Warts
These are all different possibilities. Put a small pin in the earth to rust. Steal a piece of beef and bury it. Rub the warts with a black slug, then impale it on a thorn. Gather some ripe ears of wheat and cross the wart with them several times; then put the corn into a packet and drop it where three roads meet. Cut as many notches in a stick as there are warts, and drop it where four roads meet.

Secretly pinch out of a loaf of bread as many pieces as there are warts and bury them. Cut as many notches as there are warts in two sticks; lay them crosswise in the road, and the warts will be taken by whoever picks up the sticks. Make the sign of the cross and repeat *Gloria Patri* (Glory be to the Father)—though this can be done only by someone with the gift of charming. Sell them. (I met in 1990 a Bromyard doctor who said that he had often bought warts from patients).

## Wen

Arrange for the wen, a lump or protuberance on the body, to be touched by the hand of a dead man. (Hands from executed criminals were severed, then pickled for the purpose.)

## Whooping Cough

Here again there are many different options. Eat bread and butter which has been placed in a dead man's hand. Take 20 hairs from the nape of the patient's neck (or seven from the tail of a white horse) and put them between slices of bread and butter; give this sandwich to the first strange dog which passes, and say the Lord's Prayer; the dog will carry away the disease. Hold a frog in the mouth of the patient and cause him to breathe into its mouth; the frog will take away the disease. Inhale the breath of a piebald horse. Pass the patient nine mornings running under the arch made by a bramble rooted at both ends; say the Lord's Prayer, eat some bread and butter, and give some to a bird or animal. Cause the patient to drink from a sacramental cup or eat from a bowl of ivy wood. Tie a string with nine knots round the neck. Find a married couple called Mary and Joseph and send them an unsolicited gift or ask the wife to lay her hands on the patient. Find a woman successively married to two men of the same surname but of different families; ask her to cut bread and butter and give it to the patient. Find a woman with a second husband whose surname is the same as her maiden name; anything she suggests will produce a cure, though in practice bread and butter with sugar was usually recommended.

## Weather Lore

Before the days of scientific weather forecasting people amassed a whole host of predictions, some general, some particular, which were the fruit of generations of knowledge. Many provide sound advice, particularly when they describe the sky itself, though none works all the time. For example, 'Rain before seven, dry before eleven' often proves true because most frontal rain bands last only a few hours; however, we can all remember occasions when rain has continued for a whole day or even longer. To take a different instance, the traditional view (see below) that January is the 'blackest' month is confirmed by scientific evidence that it is indeed, on average, the coldest month of the year in most places in the British Isles. On the other hand, the calendar changes of 1752 and also variations in climate such as the global warming we are beginning to experience affect the accuracy of any weather lore of long standing. The easiest traditional observations to dismiss are those connected with miracle-working saints such as Swithin (for whom, see below). Weather lore was often cast into rhyme to make it easily memorable.

The moon was believed to be a very useful indicator. For example, the appearance of a new moon on a Saturday would bring twenty days of wind and rain. Put another way:

> If the moon on a Saturday be new or full,
> There always was rain and there always wull.

On the other hand, 'Sunday's Moon comes too soon', that is, a new moon on a Sunday brings ill fortune. A moon on its back brings dry weather: 'Moon on its back holds water in its lap' but if the points are downward rain is indicated.

We are still preoccupied with rain, both in timing and in quantity, and there are probably more traditional sayings on this subject than any other. 'When the sun sets in a muddy mist, be sure that rain's at hand', is how one expression puts it. A local variant of the old shepherd's rhyme goes: 'A rainbow at night is the shepherd's delight'. A more elaborate verse runs:

> When the reds are out at night it's the shepherd's delight,
> But when out in the morning it's all day storming.

Several signs of rain were known at Weobley. Jackdaws circling the church spire gave one. Another was when the wind blew in 'Weobley hole'. A third concerned a high, tree-covered hill:

> When Lady Lift puts on her shift
> She fears a downright rain,
> But when she doffs it you will find
> The rain is o'er, and still the wind,
> And Phoebus shines again.

Still current is the belief that the appearance of black beetles points to rain— and if they are killed it will be all the wetter. A cock's crow can also be significant:

> A cock crowing on going to bed,
> Sign he'll get up with a dropping [dripping] head.

*Lady Lift Hill above Weobley*

The well known rhyme about the oak and ash is often thought to mean that we shall have rain either way, but a local variant makes clear that this is not so:

> If the oak be out before the ash
> There'll only be a little splash;
> If the ash be out before the oak
> Then there'll be a regular soak.

Another sign from a tree relates not to weather but to fishing:

> When the bud of the orl [alder] is as big as a trout's eye,
> Then that fish is in season in the River Wye.

The best of the weather lore derived from a careful reading of the sky and the winds. 'Cruddledy [curdled] sky, cruddledy sky, not long wet, not long dry', says one forecast. Others predict 'Cloudy mornings turn to clear evenings' and 'Dew before midnight, next day will be bright'. The wind features in 'The weather's always ill when the wind's not still' and 'When the wind is in the east, there it will be for some days at least'. As winter approaches 'A storm of hail brings frost in its tail'. Even onions can provide predictions:

> Onion skins very thin,
> A mild winter coming in.
> Onion skins thick and tough,
> Coming winter wild and rough.

Most months of the year have their own lore. People were reluctant to settle bills on 1 January since they believed: 'Pay away money on New Year's Day, all the year through you'll have money to pay'. The same day had a rhyme about the lengthening of light:

> At New Year's tide a cock's stride;
> By Twelfth-tide another beside.

At Upton Bishop the second line was varied to 'Candlemas an hour's tide'. Twelfth-tide, or 6 January, was also known after the change of calendar in 1752 as Old Christmas Day; on this occasion one should rejoice if the sun shines through the branches of the apple trees.

On the whole January was not a popular month. 'As the days lengthen the cold strengthens' can still be heard, though perhaps not 'The blackest month of all the year, it is the month of Janiveer'. A mild January was thought to bring a cold May, though it was considered good time for planting at least one crop: 'Who in January sows oats, gets gold and groats'.

The weather on Candlemas Day (2 February) seems to have been very carefully watched for its predictive qualities. If the wind was in the west at midday it was thought to portend a good year for fruit. Wherever the wind was, especially in the east, there it would 'abide till the second of May' (or, in another adage, until May Eve). Still at Candlemas, geese should begin laying. A farmer should still have half his straw and half his hay because a good deal of the winter might still be to come. 'Never come Lent, never come winter' means that one cannot rely that winter is over till Lent is past. If the birds sang before Candlemas (or alternatively, on Candlemas Day) they would cry before May. The message is given with greater clarity in this verse:

> If Candlemas Day be dark and black
> It will carry cold winter away on its back,
> But if Candlemas Day be bright and clear
> The half of winter's to come this year.

'A February spring is worth nothing' seems another way of expressing the second couplet. 'February grass wipes March's arse' is taken to mean that a flush of grass in a mild February is always checked by bad weather in March. More optimistically, 'Much February snow a fine summer doth show'.

'Never come March, never come winter' was an expression used until at least the 1960s at Much Marcle. The feeling that winter is not yet over is also reflected in:

> March will search and April try
> But May will tell if you live or die.

The winds of this month were regarded as significant:

> If the wind is in the east at noon on St. Benedict's Day [21 March],
> It will neither chop nor change till the end of May.

One rhyme was peculiar to the people of Ledbury:

> If the March wind blows to Ross [that is from the north-east]
> The fruit crop will be a loss.
> If the March wind blows to Worcester [that is from the south-west]
> All fruit will hang in clusters.

A general comment on fruit growing runs:

> March dust on the apple leaf
> Brings all kind of fruit to grief.

In other words, a wet March does good; but opinions differ, for another saying claims 'A peck of March dust is worth a king's ransom'. One more rhyme to complete March's story:

> If the apple trees bloom in March
> For barrels of cider you need not sarch;
> If the apple trees bloom in May
> You can eat apple dumplings every day.

The theme of cider making was taken up in April:

> When apple trees are in blossom in April and before May
> You can put all your barrels away,
> But if they blossom at the end of May and the beginning of June
> You can get all your barrels in tune.

Other sayings for the month include 'A cold April, the barn will fill' and 'If it thunder on All Fools' Day, it brings good crops of grass and hay'. However, 'April oats and August hay, weeds the farmer's living away'; the implication here is that the oats are planted and the hay gathered too late. A parallel rhyme runs 'Cuckoo oats and orchard hay, make a farmer run away', the oats having been sown too late, the hay being too difficult to cut.

*The Boot Inn, Orleton*

In Herefordshire the cuckoo came to the cattle fair once held on 23 April at the Boot Inn, Orleton; there she bought a horse, and went to Bron (Brampton Bryan) Fair on 22 June to sell him. No doubt the coincidences of the cuckoo's coming and going with these events led to the belief. Incidentally, the expression 'gone to Bron Fair' was used of peas and other crops which looked weakly.

'Easter come early, Easter come late, it's sure to make the old cow quake' gives warning that bad weather is still to be expected at this time of year. Another prediction seems to show that plenty will grow but little will be gathered in:

> If the sun shines through the trees on Easter Day
> We shall have a good year of grass and a poor one of hay.

The same is said of Christmas Day and also—with regard to hops—of Good Friday.

'A cold May is kind' recalls the rhyme about the benefit of a cold April. On the other hand, 'A May wet was never kind yet'; but there are, as always, other views: 'A wet and windy May, and the barns are full of hay' or 'A warm and dappledy May, the barns are full of hay'.

To ensure successive crops runner beans should be planted on May Eve and June Eve. In South Herefordshire the people believed in planting swedes at the time of Coleford Fair (9 June). The classic formula for bean planting is:

When elmen leaves are big as a shilling,
Plant kidney beans if to plant 'em you're willing.
When elmen leaves are as big as a farden,
Plant kidney beans in your garden.
When elmen leaves are as big as a penny,
Plant kidney beans if you mean to have any.

Apart from the lack of elm leaves to observe, this rhyme is now surely doomed to fall out of use through the disappearance of the farthing and the old penny.

The rhyme about the value of swarms of bees in different months remains very well known, but the one about thistles is less so:

Cut thistles in May,
They grow in a day.
Cut them in June,
That is too soon.
Cut them in July,
Then they will die.

The weather in May and June was rightly seen to have its effect on the coming harvest. 'Mist in May and heat in June will bring the harvest very soon', was one prediction. Contrariwise, another said 'A dry May and a dripping June always brings things in tune'. St. Barnabas' Day (11 June) signalled the beginning of haymaking: 'On Saint Barnabas put the scythe to grass'. Rain was expected to christen the apples on St. Peter's Day (29 June).

Many country people still hold to the opinion that if rain falls on St. Swithin's Day (15 July) it will continue for forty days. The belief has over a thousand years of history behind it, but no weight of metereological evidence. Indeed, it was announced in 2001 that in that year and the previous 54 the prediction had proved wrong. When Swithin died in 862 he left instructions that he was to be buried outside the west door of the Old Minster at Winchester. This was done, but about a hundred years later a decision was taken to move his remains inside the cathedral. On the day in question—15 July 971—miraculous cures were effected but heavy rain began to fall and lasted for 40 days.

*Apple-picking at Dorstone in ?1940s*

The period from August to November seems less rich in weather lore, perhaps because after harvest at least the weather was not so important. Michaelmas (29 September) occasioned the wry reflection that plentiful supplies of apples would not last for ever:

> At Michaelmas or a little before,
> Half the apple's thrown away with the core.
> At Christmas time or a little bit arter
> If it's as sour as a crab,
> It's 'Thank you, master'.

In October farmers put rams to their ewes: 'At St. Luke's Day [18 October] let tups have play'. In November signs of winter started to be seen:

> Ice in November to hold a duck,
> There follows a winter of slush and muck.

However, if the first snow of the season hung in the trees it was thought to indicate that the following year would be good for fruit. A similar sign was that if the sun shone through the orchard on Christmas Day a good year for apples would ensue. The same weather unfortunately predicted many fires in the year. Other signs were: 'Hours of sun on Christmas Day, so many frosts in the month of May' and 'If Christmas Day be bright and clear, there'll be two winters in the year'.

The day on which Christmas fell had its significance:

> If Christmas on a Thursday be
> A windy winter you shall see:
> Windy days in every week,
> Winter weather strong and thick;
> Summer shall be good and dry,
> Corn and wheat shall multiply.

An alternative was that if Christmas Day fell on a Sunday the following summer would be hot. Finally, and somewhat lugubriously, 'A green Christmas means a full churchyard'.

# CHAPTER 6

# The Supernatural

The supernatural has been a very long time a-dying. Although fairies are now largely confined to children's books and films, belief in them among adults lingered until the earlier part of the last century. Similarly, the physical presence of the devil was accepted by many until well within living memory.

The witch with her cat, broomstick and spells might now seem to belong only to the fantasy of Disney films or the horror of cult videos, yet she has a long and perhaps unfinished history. There are written records of Amisia Daniel, 'the Cradley witch', who lived on Wild Goose Hill, Storridge, between 1397 until 1400, but she remains a shadowy figure. Almost six hundred years later the planned re-enactment of a witch burning as part of the commemoration of a Civil War battle at Ledbury in 1991 was called off after a protest. The organiser commented: 'We were contacted by a witch who said it was very distasteful to hold a burning ceremony so we cancelled it rather than offend anyone'. Such mildness would have seemed very strange a few hundred years ago when witches faced the death penalty for their activities, and more recently still, when they were hated and feared by their neighbours.

Such fears of witches and the Wild Hunt—spirits of the restless dead riding through the sky and presaging calamity—may now have diminished, but the notion that in some circumstances the spirits of the dead return to their erstwhile surroundings is undoubtedly persistent. The perturbation in life—violence, injustice, sin of omission or commission—which causes ghosts to walk is sometimes well documented, sometimes mysterious.

**Fairies**
Late in the nineteenth century John Masefield was being shown fairy rings on a hill near Ledbury—he does not say which. Until at least the 1920s small clay pipes found by people digging their gardens were called 'fairy pipes'. Roman coins unearthed at Bolitree (*Ariconium*) were known as 'fairies' money'. The same was true of Kenchester (*Magna Castra*), where in the time of Leland

ruins included 'The King of the Fairies' Chair'. The little people were thought to dance round it on moonlit nights.

Place names referring to Puck, Hob or Dob—all beneficent and occasionally mischievous spirits—are widespread. They include Dobbin's Meadow (Mathon) and Pokehouse Wood (Aymestrey), where a man bequeathed money to provide for a bell to guide benighted travellers (see chapter 3) after being led astray by Puck in the guide of a will o' the wisp.

People tried hard to befriend the fairies, who could inspire fear. They were able to spoil butter, to steal babies and substitute changelings, to inveigle people into accompanying them for what seems a few minutes or hours and turned out to be years. They rode borrowed horses on moonlit nights, the evidence for which was that the animals would be found first thing in the morning dishevelled and sweating in their stables.

Until the twentieth century stories were told such as this, related to Mrs. Leather in 1910 by a seventy-five year old woman from Wigmore:

> She said it happened to her mother's first cousin ..., a girl about eighteen, [who] was very fond of dancing: she insisted on going to all the balls for miles around: whenever there was dancing going on, there was she. Her people told her something would happen to her some day, and one night when she was coming home just by the 'Dancing Gates', near Kington, she heard beautiful music. It was the music of the fairies, and she was caught into the ring. Search was made for her, and she appeared to her friends from time to time, but when they spoke to her she immediately disappeared. Her mother was told (probably by the wise man or woman), that if seen again she must be very quickly seized, without speaking, or she would never come back. So one day, a year after her disappearance, her mother saw her, and took hold of her dress before she could escape. 'Why mother', she said, 'where have you been since yesterday?' The time must have gone merrily with her, for the year had seemed but one day.
>
> The girl was none the worse, however, and they sent her to serve at a small shop in Kington. Before long the fairies came there, and used to steal little things off the counter. Afraid that she might be accused when the things were missed, the girl told her employer. 'How can you see the fairies?' he said, 'They are invisible'. She told him that when she lived with them they used a kind of ointment, and she rubbed a little of it on one eye, to try the effect. She afterwards warned the fairies that their thefts were discovered; they were much puzzled to find themselves visible to her. She was careful not to explain lest they might try to damage the eye with which she could see them.

## The Devil

Many people disliked to name the devil or the fairies. They preferred Old Nick, 'the old 'un' or simply 'him' for the one, and 'the little people', 'the pharisees' or 'them' for the others. In former times, though, feelings went well beyond vague unease to downright fear.

A demon—if not the devil himself—is said to have turned up in Hereford Cathedral in about 1290. He was beaten over the head for his trouble, and locked up. The treatment is somewhat curious for a creature supposedly possessing satanic powers, but perhaps reassuring to anyone hearing the story.

Some four centuries later, John Aubrey recorded an amusing incident involving the mathematician, Thomas Allen (who died in 1632):

> One time being at Hom Lacy in Herefordshire, at Mr. John Scudamore's (grandfather to the Lord Scudamore) he happened to leave his Watch in the Chamber windowe. (Watches were then rarities). The maydes came in to make the Bed, and hearing a thing in a case cry Tick, Tick, Tick, presently concluded that that was his Devill, and tooke it by the String with the tongues [tongs], and threw it out of the windowe into the Mote (to drowne the Devill). It so happened that the string hung on a sprig of elder that grew out of the Mote, and this confirmed them 'twas the Devill. So the good old Gentleman gott his Watch again.

The notion of demonic possession may have crossed the mind of Rev. George Powell, rector of Dorstone for 47 years until his retirement in 1953, when Lucy Probert of Scar Cottage complained that chairs and tables were thrown round her rooms, and her bed was shaken so that 'it do make my teeth rattle'. Rev. Powell visited the house, prayed and read *Matthew* 4: 23-4: 'And Jesus went all about Galilee, teaching in their synagogues, and preaching the gospel of the kingdom, and healing all manner of sickness and all manner of disease among the people. And his fame went throughout all Syria: and they brought unto him all sick people that were taken with divers diseases and torments,

*The devil attempting a seduction, from a medieval woodcut*

and those which were possessed with devils, and those which were lunatick, and those that had the palsy; and he healed them'. The disturbances at Scar Cottage ceased.

Many place names are associated with the devil. Devil's Wood is to be found on the north side of Orcop Hill. It is also known as Fairy Ring or Poor Man's Wood, and may have been a grove sacred to the Silures in which human life was sacrificed. A local belief was that if the wood were felled the owner of the Mynde, a mansion at Much Dewchurch, or his heir, would die within the year. A variation is that the prohibition refers only to a certain stump, or merely to wych hazels and wych elms. One wych elm on the Witches' Tump in the grounds of the house is said to mark the spot where a witch was burnt. The wood's evil influence has been blamed for a series of misfortunes stretching over two hundred years up to 1948 at Symons Farm. One explanation for these stories is that before the Reformation a curse was placed on the owners of the Mynde for alienating the wood from the poor of the parish to whom it had been bequeathed. Another is that Poor Man is a euphemism for the devil, whose writ still runs through the wood.

The Devil's Garden is part of the Stanner Rocks, near Kington, where nothing will grow. In Kington itself a dissolute tailor made a suit for the devil but took fright at the last moment and declined to take any payment. Afterwards he became a model of good behaviour. A friar at Stoke Edith was less fortunate. In a wood he spotted the devil in the guise of a badger, but the badger carried off the friar.

Still at Stoke Edith— which for all its small size seems to be full of tradi- tions—you could see the devil if you walked seven times round the church, then looked through the keyhole. Neighbouring Tarrington had a similar belief; there the ritual included saying the

*Stoke Edith Church*

Lord's Prayer backwards. This was the case, too, at Weobley, where one had to walk seven times backwards round each tier of steps on the preaching cross in the church-yard. The feat has been tried many times, but apparently without success. On one occasion at Weobley, though, boys at the school managed to raise the devil by following a formula they found in a book of their master which they consulted in his absence. Having conjured the devil they were unable to get rid of him, but the scandalised schoolmaster did the trick on his return. What he did to the pupils afterwards was not recorded.

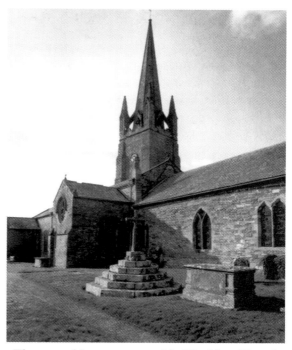

*The preaching cross outside Weobley Church*

At Dorstone a ne'er-do-well called Jack of France happened to look through the keyhole of the church door on the eve of All Souls' Day (2 November). He saw the devil in the pulpit, dressed as a monk, and heard him reading the names of those who were to die in the ensuing year. Jack's name was on the list. He went home, took to his bed, and died.

Such fears are now forgotten, but some still tell children not to pick black-berries after 29 September because on that day the devil spits on them.

## Witchhunts

Witches were pursued by both church and state because they were thought to worship the devil. The last trial for witchcraft in Hereford took place in 1712, but the heyday for prosecutions was the previous century. Patchy court docu-ments mean that some cases went unrecorded, while in others the sentences are not known. Witches' confessions—often extracted under torture or the threat of it—were remarkably similar. No doubt reflecting what interrogators wished to hear, they included impossible feats like flying through the air and improbable deeds such as having sexual intercourse with the devil.

One test applied to a suspected witch was to bind the woman's limbs and throw her into water. The innocent sank; the guilty 'swam', or floated. An inci-dent at Upton Bishop in 1849 involved a punitive ducking rather than a water test. Hannah Goode, who lived at Hill Top, had the reputation of being a witch. A crowd one day surrounded her house with the intention of making her ride the stang—an ash pole decorated with stinging nettles and a ram's skull—to the nearest pond. When she came to the door she was stoned. A number of arrests were made, which led to fines of 2s. 6d. per person, with costs of 6s. 6d.

As early as 1397 the bishop of Hereford was informed that whenever Alison Brown of Bromyard uttered a curse God always put it into effect. There is a record that in about 1598 John Smyth cursed William Walton of Yarpole, 'kneeling on his knees in the churchyard there, and upon him and all his cattle'. A similar ritual was followed by Joanna Nurden when she cursed John Sergeant and his wife at Much Marcle in 1616; and in 1655 Rachel Dewsall of Hereford 'pulled up her clothes and kneeled down upon her bare knees and cursed her son and daughter and wished they might never prosper'. Five years later a citizen of Hereford, Philip Benny, alleged that he knew Mary Hodges was plotting against someone because at bedtime:

> she is observed to take the andirons out of the chimney, and put them cross one another and then she falls down on her knees and useth some prayers of witchcraft. ... She then makes water in a dish and throws it upon the said andirons and then takes her journey into her garden. This is her usual custom night after night.

One smiles at reading such things until one remembers that they could have led to a horrible death for an alleged witch. Witchcraft ceased to be a legal offence in 1736 but its shadow lay over people for perhaps another two hundred years.

## Strange powers

Near Mansell Lacy a witch stopped a team of horses and agreed to lift the spell only when the carter threatened her with his whip. This might have been made of elder or mountain ash, both of which are feared by witches. The same woman put a spell on an old farmer so that he was powerless to go beyond a certain house on the edge of the village, nor could his horse pass the spot. The man used to wait there while his children posted letters in the village or collected what he wanted. Eventually there was such an outcry that the vicar went to the witch's house and burnt all her books, thus sapping her power. All this occurred in the 1840s.

A more recent incident was remembered by an inmate of Ross workhouse and told to Mrs. Leather:

> He was coming over Whitney Bridge, many years ago, when behind the cart he was driving came a waggoner with three horses, and no money to pay toll. He defied the old woman at the toll house, and would have

driven past her, but she witched the horses so that they would not move. 'I sin it meself, them 'orses 'ouldn't muv nor stir, and when I lent the mon the toll money they went right on through. There was funny tales about that old 'ooman: folks took care they didna give her offence: 'er'd make their pigs dance in their cots till they fetched her to stop 'em.

At Leigh Sinton hounds kept by a Mr. Spooner would always start unseen game in a particular field called the Oak and Crab Tree Ground. The dogs would pursue the quarry but invariably lose it on Crampton Hill at Cradley by a cottage belonging to an old woman called Cofield. A similar tale, often told in Herefordshire, relates how as hounds scent a hare a little boy's voice is heard shouting 'Run, granny, run. The dogs be arter ee'. As the hare bounds through a hedge to safety one of the hounds manages to bite its hind leg. A few minutes later a huntsman knocks at a cottage door to ask whether the hare has been seen, and he finds an old woman bathing a fresh wound in her leg.

Liza Lloyd of Commonbach, Dorstone, is still remembered as a witch because she was born with only three fingers on each hand. Women such as she could inspire fear. It was believed that the Scudamores of Holme Lacy had been punished by a curse that direct heirs to the estate would always die before their fathers. This happened twice. At Dorstone a farmer seduced his servant girl but refused to marry her when she became pregnant. She went to America with her baby, leaving behind a solemn curse. A rector's wife commented: 'Certainly, ill luck has in that case followed this man; his children without exception have

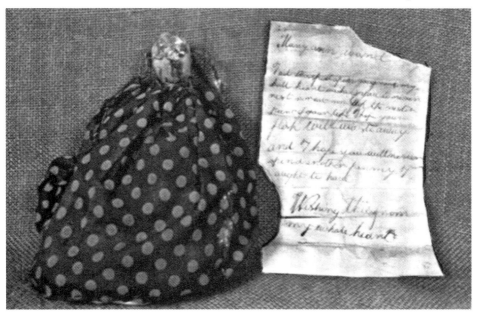

*A doll with its curse, Hereford City Museum*

*Wooden coffin with effigy, Hereford City Museum*

died or behaved ill, his crops fail and his cattle die, though he is sober and fastidious'.

In Hereford Museum is a curse doll of the late nineteenth century found in 1960 at 21 East Street in the city. A paper with it bears these words:

> Mary Ann Ward
> I act this spell upon you from my holl heart wishing you to never rest nor eat nor sleep the rest part of your life I hope your flesh will waste away and I hope you will never spend another penny I ought to have Wishing this from my whole heart

The identity of the person issuing the curse is not known.

Another item in the museum, also from the nineteenth century, is a little wooden coffin with a human effigy, the body firmly pinned down by a nail. This was found only in 1987 at a house in the village of Woolhope. Soon after it came to light the lady of the house was visiting friends when an entire window fell on her from three stories up. Fortunately she was dealt only a glancing blow but she could easily have been killed. Then her daughter became mysteriously ill, and the lady decided to rid herself of the object by taking it to Hereford Museum. The curator kept it in her office for a short time and almost immediately her husband was involved in a serious car accident. She hastily moved it to the more impersonal surroundings of a display case, where it can currently be seen.

## Some Precautions

Walter Map (see below) tells of a sorcerer in a Welsh border town who would not rest in the grave after his death. Each night he came back and called on one or two of his former neighbours, who then fell ill and died within three days. When this had gone on for some time an English knight, Sir Walter Laudun, approached Gilbert Foliot, bishop of Hereford, for advice. He was told to dig up the body, behead it, douse it with holy water, and then re-bury it. The instructions were carried out but they had no effect. One night Sir Walter heard his own name called by the sorcerer. He jumped up, snatched his sword and ran after the living corpse. Before it could return to the grave he cut off its head. Only then did the reign of terror end.

A less dramatic way of controlling witches was to find someone with superior powers. Such a person lived betwen Hereford and Bromyard during the second half of the nineteenth century. Mrs. Leather, who was told many tales of his exploits, is deliberately vague as to where he lived, and calls him Jenkins only to conceal his real name. Perhaps she wished to avoid giving offence to relatives still alive when she was writing.

Jenkins, known as 'maister o' the witches', became so well known that he was brought before the magistrates for imposture. He claimed that he indeed had power over witches. The magistrates said they did not exist. Jenkins, offering to convince them, asked whether they would prefer him to produce them in a high wind or a low wind. They declined either alternative.

One of Jenkin's exploits is attributed in a different account to a farmer from Preston Wynne. Perhaps he and the farmer were the same person. The man was renowned for his ability to remove spells. He also had second sight, and people travelled long distances to see him. Once he visited the Buck Inn (now closed) at Woonton. After the meal he called for the reckoning, and the landlady replied 'Fourpence for eat, fourpence for drink, eight pence on the whole'. Thinking the charge exorbitant, the farmer put the money on the table and drew a circle round it in chalk. When the landlady came to pick up the money she began to go round and round the table, repeating her request for payment. The servant came and tried to reach the money but the same thing happened to her. The ostler came in and tried: then there were three people circling the table. Another servant went out into the yard where the farmer was preparing to depart, and quietly asked him what was to be done. 'You take the money with a pair of tongs', he said. 'That will stop them'.

A similar situation occurs in a printed ballad entitled *The Enchanted Piss-pot* which came to light at Rhayader only in 1991 but was sold (and probably printed) in Hereford some two hundred years earlier. Here a wise man is enlisted by a farmer 'to know whether he was cuckold or no'. He sets up a spell which causes the farmer's wife and the parish clerk who is indeed cuckolding him to stick to a chamber pot and dance with it in their night attire through the town. They are released only when the clerk agrees to pay the farmer £10 in compensation.

Some people carried charms to counteract spells. Objects were often kept in the home or farm to repel witches. A horseshoe was fastened over doors or bedsteads. The coloured glass walking sticks made at Stourbridge—now kept purely as a pleasing nicknack—were once thought to protect a house against witchcraft. Another possibility was to draw a neat border of white chalk round a doorstep after it had been scrubbed, then to mark nine Xs in a row inside.

Various plants were also deemed to be effective. A house leek (*Sempervivum tectorum*) growing on a roof or wall was considered particularly good against witches—and also lightning. Twigs of wych elm or wych hazel—the latter ideally in bundles of nine—were also used, though their names are not in fact connected with witches since wych means pliant.

The mountain ash or rowan was known as 'wittan', 'wittern' or 'witty' in Herefordshire, where a saying still current in the early twentieth century ran 'the witty is the tree on which the devil hanged his mother'. 'Witty-tree and birch, say the bells of Peterchurch' is another saying associating two anti-witch trees. The red berries of the rowan were thought a good protection in themselves against evil. Goads of the wood prevented horses from being 'overlooked', and cattle were given collars of it. Yoke-pins were made of yew or rowan. At least until the 1950s some farmers nailed a sprig of rowan or birch to barn doors to keep witches away.

Elder was unlucky to cut or burn, but a branch might be nailed over a door to keep witches out. A piece of the wood was often let into churns to prevent witches from spoiling the butter.

## Persistence

The widespread use of such devices is an indication of the extent to which belief in the malevolent powers of witches continued until within living memory. Mrs. Leather was told by a Weobley man that he had gone to assist a policeman trying to arrest the drunken son of a local witch: 'I helped him and didn't think. My missis said when I came home I'd be sorry for it. Sure enough, my pig died next week'.

Certain villages were feared for their witches. 'There'll always be nine witches from the bottom of Orcop to the end of Garway Hill as long as water runs' was the firm belief in a remote area of Herefordshire. A well known witch lived at Cockyard, near Abbey Dore. One account of her was written in 1928:

> You could hear her a long way before you saw her. Her stick went thump, thump. No schoolmaster would stay long in Abbey Dore schoolhouse. Everyone gave the same reason, until a man who had failed in farming came there with two sons and two daughters. On dark nights they would

hear 'thump, thump', and steps round the house; often the windows would shake as though every pane would fall out. They would go to bed, and then they would hear such a noise, as if a dozen people were moving the chairs, and plates and dishes rattling. When they came down in the morning, everything would be as they left it. This continued for years. The old Cockyard witch died; they never heard anything after. ...

These witches had the credit of going into stables and riding the horses; these would sometimes be found in such a state that they could not be worked. The last night in April was much feared. The waggoners always put boughs of two trees—one was birch [and the other was rowan]—each side and over the stable door; wherever you went, you would see these boughs on stables. If people were killed, it was laid to the witches. We often heard of horses being found dead at different houses, three and four the same night. Now, the witches are dead.

Yet at least one witch is still feared at Cockyard, and she may be the same one which terrorised the people of Abbey Dore schoolhouse. Her name is Nanny Gunter, and she is supposed to have killed some of her children and buried them in a wood. Her name is applied in Cockyard to a stretch of road, Nanny Gunter's Pitch. To this day some people find it eerie and avoid travelling along it, even by car.

Many miles away the story of another witch is remembered. Mrs. S. Rickhuss of Ronkswood, Worcester, gave me this version of it:

I'll tell you about a tale my mother told me, she herself a country-born lass from Herefordshire. It is the legend of Jumper's Hole. There was a gamekeeper's cottage near Bromyard as you travel towards Bishops Frome, on Dovehills Farm. On the outskirts of a wood at the bottom of a bank [between Stanford Bishop and Acton Beauchamp] runs a brook and above it [is] a gate. One time a witch came down from the woods on a horse and went to the cottage to ask for a loaf of bread. It being a poor farm the owner refused her request, so she cursed the homestead and stole the bread. It is said on her way back as she jumped the brook she dropped the loaf of bread, and its remains can be seen in the stone where she landed, along with two hoofprints. Also the gate above is said to be cursed, as nothing will grow around it. The cottage, believed to harbour ill luck, fell into disrepair and was eventually demolished. The address was Dove Hills Cottage, Jumper's Hole, near Bromyard.

## The Wild Hunt

The ghostly hunt which rides through the sky on stormy nights is known in most parts of the world. Its appearance—even the mere sound of its riders and hounds—is thought to presage ill, and possibly disaster, for a community. A Saxon nobleman called Edric, who owned land in Shropshire and five manors (including Burrington) in Herefordshire, fiercely resisted the Norman invasion, in alliance with the Welsh kings, Bleddyn and Rhiwallon. Only in 1070 did he make peace with William the Conqueror, by which time the Normans had dubbed him Wild Edric. Ever since then, he and a ghostly army of horsemen were said to pass in procession across the sky whenever catastrophe threatened.

Less than a century after Edric's time, a different wild hunt story was noted by Walter Map in his book, *De Nugis Curialium* (Of courtiers' trifles). Map (*c*.1140-*c*.1209), a Herefordshire man with family at Wormsley and land at Ullingswick, was educated in Paris and had a successful career as diplomat and cleric—in the latter capacity as rector of Westbury-on-Severn in Gloucestershire and (from 1197) as archdeacon of Oxford. His book is a collection of anecdotes and tales, history and fiction, compiled between 1180 and 1193. In it he tells of Herla, a king of the ancient Britons, who was making preparations for his wedding when a pygmy king, mounted on a goat, visited him and asked to be allowed to attend. This was agreed, and Herla accepted an invitation to the pygmy's wedding to be held a year later.

On Herla's wedding day the pygmy returned with richly-dressed attendants who served food and drink in opulent vessels. He left at cock-crow after reminding Herla of their agreement. A year later he came back, and led Herla and his retinue to a cave in a cliff by the Wye. The pygmy's wedding was celebrated with great pomp, and after three days of feasting Herla left, laden with gifts which included a small bloodhound. This had to be carried until it jumped down of its own accord; no one was to dismount until then.

Outside the cave Herla met an old shepherd whom he asked for news of the queen. The man replied that he barely understood the question since his language was Saxon; the only queen of the name given that he knew was the wife of King Herla who had disappeared at the very cliff several centuries earlier.

Forgetting the injunction about the bloodhound, some of Herla's men dismounted and immediately crumbled into dust. Herla warned the rest to stay on horseback till the dog jumped down, but it never did. The cavalcade rode on through the centuries at least until the time of Henry II when it disappeared into the Wye, at last finding repose, and transferring its ceaseless quest to others.

One of the hunt's manifestations experienced in more recent years is the sound of the Seven Whistlers in the night sky (see also chapter 5). To hear six of these is an ill omen; seven at once would signal the end of the world. No one can identify these birds, which have variously been taken to be swans, wild geese, whimbrels, curlews and swifts.

## Ghosts

For reasons which remain mysterious some people seem to have been reluctant to leave their earthly haunts. The dissolution of the monasteries by Henry VIII may account for some ghostly happenings. Once in the 1920s when the oven at Abbey Farm, Craswall, was under repair the Bevans (who lived at the farm) decided one evening to heat the oven in the nearby abbey ruins. When they returned a little later to see how it was getting on they saw the figures of a man and woman standing before it with hands uplifted, as though warming themselves at the fire. They did no baking that night.

At Middleton-on-the-Hill a lady in white is to be seen sitting on Gravenor's Bridge on certain moonlit nights. In the same parish a grey lady walks close to a now derelict house. Court Farm at Snodhill is haunted by the sound of rustling silk dresses and the tapping of high heels. Among phenomena remembered in the 1990s at Eardisland were a lady on the stairs (Staick House), a strange presence (Manor House) and a ghost in a snuff box beneath the bridge over the Arrow—confined there, no doubt, after some forgotten exorcism (see below). Certain people in Kenchester have seen Roman soldiers marching past at night. One old lady now deceased insisted that they went through her house at the full moon, and another that they made a camp in her garden.

Most villages have a ghost story of some kind but some seem to have an abundance of such narratives. Such a claim might be made for Hoarwithy. A manuscript of the 1850s mentions a pool at Hoarwithy 'said to be haunted—teams [of horses] used to be frightened there at night or run away—one wagoner had his leg broken in an attempt to stop his team—& I am not sure there was not one killed for similar cause'. The pool was close to where 'the Bierless road falls into the Hereford Road'. In the opinion of a local historian, Heather Hurley, Bierless Road (which no longer exists, though its line can be traced) was a corpse way leading to a burial ground where the corpses of outcasts such as suicides, paupers and vagrants were interred.

Members of Hoarwithy Women's Institute gathered more stories in 1953 when a manuscript history of the village was compiled, many of them connected with the cell (burned down in mediaeval times) of Aconbury nunnery at King's Caple, or possibly St. Dubricius' Church of the Brethren at Llanfrother. Mr. Reg Langford of Red Rail Farm, close to an ancient ford over the Wye, told how on three occasions—once in the company of two other men—he had seen a cowled lady, dressed in white, who emerged from a wood, walked a litle way into a field, and vanished. A different encounter was related by Mr. Colin Eckley, who was riding home one afternoon on his bicycle past Tressech Farm. At a point where the road is narrow and bordered by steep banks he saw walking in front a woman in a long grey dress. He braked hard but unnecessarily for she had disappeared where even a young, athletic woman could not have escaped.

Still further sightings include 'the top half of a woman sticking out of the hedge'; a figure taken by a cyclist to be the schoolmistress on an evening stroll, but 'however hard he pedalled she was always the same distance away from him till at last she disappeared'; and a hooded figure 'like a nun, and deathly still at that, standing under the trees by the roadside where the old Roman track from the ford joins the highway, greeted by a passer-by with a cheery "Goodnight" but making never a reply or a movement'. Yet another lady is unseen by the occupants of Upper Orchard House (formerly the Harp and Anchor Inn) but perceived by visitors. One more appears from time to time on the Wye in a boat travelling far faster than wind or current could propel it.

Finally, the story noted by Rev. William Poole of a young farm lad, Tom Reece, who was walking home to Hoarwithy after a convivial evening in Ross when he became aware of a big Newfoundland dog padding along by his side. After a time Tom became annoyed with his silent companion and took a stick to the dog, which not only evaded all his blows with ease but turned into a likeness of the lad's father, who had died some weeks earlier. Tom reached home 'dead sober' and 'glum as a reaper when his bottle is empty'. He said nothing of his experiences but became depressed and morose.

One stormy February evening, he suddenly got up and announced that he must go out, telling his brother that their father had summoned him. At midnight he returned, seeming happier, but several days elapsed before he said what had happened. He went to where he had seen the dog, and his father had appeared and beckoned him to follow into a wood. There he was told to dig and though he had no spade as soon as his fingers touched the ground it seemed to open to reveal a bag. 'Take it and throw it in the Wye', came the command. Tom did as he was bid, then looked round for his father, who had disappeared. He fell down in a faint, and when he came round, made his way home. He gradually recovered his spirits, and heard no more from the 'old fellow'.

## Exorcism

A belief which lingered until the twentieth century was that money and also iron misplaced or hidden in life would prevent due repose in death. Ghosts haunt the sites of hidden treasure until it is found and their responsibility discharged. At Castle Farm, Madley, though, a ghost seems to have appeared only after a crock of gold was discovered in the cellar.

Since Biblical times the illegal moving of landmarks has been considered a great wrong. This, too, can cause a ghost to walk. Many years ago—the story was remembered in the 1870s by a nonagenarian—the White Cross, then just outside Hereford on the Brecon road, was haunted by 'Old Taylor' as a punishment for moving a landmark. One evening a local man called Dennis encountered the ghost, which persuaded him to return at midnight. Dennis related this in the Nag's Head to considerable disbelief, since he was known as an inveterate liar. He felt obliged to keep the appointment. Old Taylor led him to a huge pair of stones and asked him to move them. At first Dennis demurred at their size but discovered that after all he had the strength to shift them, as Taylor

*The tomb of Ellen and Thomas Vaughan, Kington Church*

asked. Then he was told to lie down until he heard music, at which signal he was to get away as quickly as possible. After this he was a changed man, but he did not live long. His drinking companions perhaps posthumously conceded his veracity, for Old Taylor ceased to walk.

Such results were more usually achieved after a formal ceremony of exorcism. The ghost of a grey lady on a grey horse was successfully imprisoned in a goose quill and consigned to Haugh Pool, near Yarpole. The exorcism is related in greater detail in the case of Thomas Vaughan ap Rosser, of Hergest Court, near Kington. Thomas, born in 1400 and nicknamed Black Vaughan after his dark hair or possibly his nature, married Ellen Gethin from Llanbister, just over the Welsh border in Radnorshire. Ellen was fiercely protective of her younger brother, David, and after her marriage brought him to live at Hergest Court. In 1430 David, during a visit to Llanbister, quarrelled with his cousin, John Hir, over their shares in an inheritance. Swords were drawn. David died. Ellen, 'a woman of masculine strength and intrepid spirit', determined to take revenge. Disguised in men's clothing, she went to an archery tournament at Llanddewi Ystradenni, the neighbouring parish to Llanbister, and challenged the best man there. John Hir responded and shot an arrow into the bull. When Ellen's turn came, she shot him through the heart.

Her husband died many years later during the Wars of the Roses. A supporter of the Yorkist king, Edward IV, Vaughan was marching towards Banbury in 1469 to join the battle when a Lancastrian party captured him. He was taken to Pontefract and beheaded. His body was brought back for burial at St. Mary's Church on the hill above Kington. Ellen joined him there some years later, and their tomb displays the couple's impressive alabaster effigies.

Ellen seems to have slept peacefully but the spirit of Thomas soon began to alarm the neighbourhood. In broad daylight it would upset farmers' wagons, frighten their wives by jumping up behind as they rode to market at Kington, and assume the shape of a monstrous fly to torment the horses. In the guise of a roaring bull it even charged into the church during a service. People began to avoid the town, and its prosperity suffered.

Some four hundred years after the event, a local molecatcher gave this account to Kilvert:

> Twelve or thirteen ancient parsons assembled in the court of Hergest, and drew a circle, inside which they all stood with books and lighted candles, praying. The ghost was very resolute, and came among the parsons roaring like a bull. 'Why so fierce, Mr Vaughan?' asked one of the parsons mildly. 'Fierce I was a man, fiercer still as a devil', roared Vaughan, and all the candles were blown out except one, held by a very small, weak parson (also, says legend, named Vaughan). He hid the candle in his boots and so kept it alight, all the time praying hard until at length the violent spirit was quelled, 'and brought down so small and humble that they shut him up in a snuff box'. The ghost made one humble petition—'Do not bury me beneath water'. But the parson immediately had him enclosed in a stone box, and buried him under the bed of the brooks and Hergest thenceforth was at peace.

Not so. Hergest Court was haunted by a black dog which made an appearance every time a member of the Vaughan family was to die. Conan Doyle visited Hergest Court and, transposing the spectral beast to Dartmoor, created *The Hound of the Baskervilles*. (Both Doyle and the Vaughans were connected by marriage to the Baskerville family.)

A contributor to the Woolhope Society *Transactions* wrote in 1940 that an attempt 'some years ago' failed to move a large stone underneath which Black Vaughan was supposed to be confined in the pool at Hergest Court. 'Vaughan's ghost appears at night close by', he added, 'and horses have been known to refuse to pass the spot'. The daughter of the present owner told me that he conceived a plan to fill in the pool, but changed his mind when, with JCBs lined up ready on the appointed day, the water began to bubble ominously. In 1987 a Solihull woman, coincidentally called Miss Jenny Vaughan, saw the ghostly figure of a bull in the church, outlined against the blue curtain covering the

*Hergest Court and the finally drained pool in 2001*

north door. 'What struck me most', she said, 'was the incongruity of seeing a bull in a church'.

Later, the owner of Hergest Court must have had a change of heart. Late in 2001 the pool had clearly been remodelled by heavy machinery, and largely drained, to await replenishment by the winter's rain. Yet part of it, by design or accident remained under water.

Perhaps the last case of a full-blown exorcism dates from sometime between 1828 and 1854 when Rev. William Copeland was the rector of Acton Beauchamp. The ghost, that of the 'first wife of Hodges as used to have the blacksmithing at Acton Cross', was confined in Amstell Pool. Captain Andrew Haggard (1894-1977) was told the story in 1920:

> Mrs. Hodges dies and leaves two children, and the blacksmith marries again and very quick he did too—warn't that so, George?—and her was bad to children of first wife. And first wife's sperrit took to haunting her children, not tarrifying them as you might say but just standing at their beds. And the children they warn't frightened neither, 'cos you see her had her clothes on [that is, was not in her shroud]. But her come that strong that all the place was talking on it. And they tells parson and he lays un and says—parson say he don't never want no such job again— fair made him sweat it did. Copeland, yes, Copeland were parson then. And he got eleven other parsons so there was twelve on 'em each with a lit candle and they starts to read her small. Least they raised un first 'cos

with sperrits you got to raise un afore you falls un. And her come that big and the lights went out and last there was only one candle left, and fortunate that candle kept burning else she'd a bested 'em. And they got reading her smaller and smaller and got her real small and pushed un in a matchbox and throwed un in Amstell Pond as I was telling you, and her aren't troubled no one since, ent that so, George? Ah.

The Anglican church still nominates one clergyman in each diocese to carry out exorcisms as required, but there is no set form for the procedure. Alternative assistance might come from spiritualists such as John Cuninghame, who in 1998 offered to rid Eastnor Castle of thirteen ghosts. This surprised Mrs. Sarah Harvey-Bathurst, who said 'I've never been aware of any ghosts in the castle, apart from changes of atmosphere'. Ghostbusters or 'ghost detectives' were trying in 2000 to help the occupants of 53 High Street, Ross, who had been perturbed by three phantom manifestations one of which consisted of heavy breathing. Four years earlier a family living in a flat in the Newton Farm district of Hereford was driven out by poltergeist activity which included objects flying round the rooms, pictures falling from the walls, curtains opening and closing, and the television set being turned on and off. In addition the figure of a white lady flitted round the bedrooms at night. The tenants reported these phenomena to Hereford City's housing department, whose officials referred the case to the South Wye ministry team. Rev. Richard Green commented that such problems were 'quite common'. The outcome went unreported.

Such stories seem to be abundant. In 1992 a couple bought a house in Hereford and found some old-fashioned clothes in the attic which they threw out. They then started to hear a child crying. They consulted an archivist at the

*Eastnor Castle from a post card of the early 1900s*

to H.S. Boyd at Wodland Lodge, Malvern: 'I have heard no more about the ghost—excepting that now she has not merely a "local Habitation" but a name, for she is said and devoutly believed to be, Lady Tempest, who was the proprietress of this house, before Papa bought it. I hope she may keep to the bridge and not show any other local attachments'.

Another tragic love story which resulted in a ghost dates from the fourteenth century. During the reign of Edward II, Despenser, one of the king's favourites met and fell in love with Isobel Chandos, daughter of the governor of Hereford Castle. Despenser did not reveal his identity to Isobel, but one evening he warned her that there was to be a surprise attack on the castle, and implored her to leave with him. It seems that she preferred to warn her father. The attack failed. Despenser was captured and hanged in High Town. So runs the story, but the only Despenser who fits into the period in question was executed in 1326 at Bristol. Isobel, who had unwittingly betrayed him, was unhinged by grief. She took to rowing alone on the Wye, and on one of her outings she drowned. Her ghost now rows down the same stretch of river, coming ashore where she used to meet Despenser. It weeps and wails, then returns the way it came, disappearing before it reaches the city. Ill fortune comes to any who see it.

Hellens House at Much Marcle was the home in the sixteenth century of the Walwyn family (whose name still adorns one of the local public houses). Young

*Hellens*

Hetty Walwyn ran away with a lover and returned years later with nothing but a diamond ring he had given her. She was allowed back only on condition that she accept a form of solitary confinement for the rest of her life. Her room with its barred windows can still be seen, together with the bell she used to ring for attention. It is not clear whether her ghost is among the many which walk at Hellens. Servants once refused to stay in the house because of the hauntings. Early in the twentieth century a young naval lieutenant was disturbed several times one night by what he took to be a poor old lunatic clad in a long, dark dressing gown with a hood, who kept running backwards and forwards.

During the Second World War a chiropodist, Miss Sidebottom, who is described as a 'no-nonsense person', attended two ladies at Hellens. One day she found the front door open, and went in. On the stairs she met a nun coming down, and asked where the ladies were. The nun swept past, making no reply. On reaching Lady Eleanor Miss Sidebottom enquired after the guest, and received the reply 'That's no guest. It's our ghost'.

Still at Hellens is the case of a monk allegedly killed there by Parliamentary soldiers during the Civil War. The room where this happened has a chilly atmosphere and indelible bloodstains. A dog belonging to a lady personally known to me would never enter it.

Accidental deaths abound but only certain particularly striking or poignant cases seem to have produced ghosts. John Masefield heard tell of the ghosts of a coachman and guard who were killed when their stagecoach crashed on Chance's Pitch. It is strange that the thousands of road accidents which have since happened in the two counties seem to have produced no further ghosts.

Aylton Court in a tiny village near Ledbury was the home in the 1850s of a farming family called Foulger. In 1855 little Emma Foulger, aged 14, was going down the main stairs just as her older brother was coming in the front door on his way home from a shooting expedition. He stumbled, and his still-loaded gun went off. Emma was killed on the stairs, and her ghost subsequently returned to the spot. A macabre sequel to the story is that her body was stolen from its grave in the churchyard at Aylton by resurrectionists.

Violent death seems to leave a kind of supernatural legacy, at least in a few cases. The picturesque Rhydspence Inn at Whitney-on-Wye, apart from the tale

*Aylton Court*

*The Rhydspence Inn*

of a landlady who witched drovers' cattle to the spot until they paid for their overnight stay, has the story of a ferryman crossing the river from Hay, late one night, when he was stabbed to death for the sake of the accumulated pennies for fares which he kept in a jug. The thieves, spending the night at the Rhydspence, hid the pot in their room but it 'clattered and shook like like an old 'ooman' to such an extent that the robbers confessed their crime, and were later hanged at Hay.

Religious differences led in 1861 to the murder of a protestant magistrate, Robert Pye of the Mynde, by a catholic neighbour, Charles Bodenham, on whom he was trying to serve a summons. The deed took place at Bryngwyn House, Much Dewchurch, near a big walnut tree, and thereafter two figures were seen in ghostly struggle at the spot.

A farm at Weobley was haunted by 'Old Griggs' ghost' until this was shut in a silver snuffbox and dropped in a pond in Garnstone Park. Because of his tyrannical meanness Griggs was poisoned by his own grown-up children by means of cooked toads which they said were chicken livers. He took revenge by returning in the form of a calf which incessantly bleated round the house at nights, and vanished when approached. The murderers eventually abandoned the house, and it fell into ruin.

Murderers at Longtown in the far west of Herefordshire were brought to justice by suprahuman means. Two brothers killed a shepherd on the Black Mountain but before he died he prophesied that the crows would speak out and reveal the crime. Undeterred, the brothers went ahead, and then buried the body on the mountain. When the corpse was discovered there was no evidence to link them with it, but whenever the brothers went out crows came croaking round their heads. Exasperated beyond measure, one finally said to the other 'Do you remember what the poor shepherd said before we killed him on the mountain?' The remark was overheard, and led to their both being hanged. The story seems, alas, no longer to be known in the locality.

In the early nineteenth century Callow Farm which stands near the church at Callow Hill, not far from Hereford, was a coaching inn. Over a period of time travellers staying overnight at the inn disappeared. Eventually there was an enquiry; it was discovered that they had been murdered, and presumably robbed. The bodies had been carried across two fields to a house where they were buried. The house, subsequently demolished, re-appeared in ghostly fashion. In addition phantom figures carrying a heavy burden were seen crossing the fields towards it.

Existing public houses seldom seem reluctant to publicise their ghosts. The Queens Arms in Broad Street, Hereford, boasts the spectre of a Saxon warrior in its snug. The Lough Pool at Sellack has the rather more subtle scent of lavender left by a friendly but unseen ghost who moves a particular chair in one corner of the restaurant, perhaps to a place favoured in life. Mr. Graham Wilkinson, landlord in 1999 of the refurbished Crown Inn at the Lea, soon learned local stories: 'On cold winter mornings, when it's misty, you can hear carriages as they come up Cut Throat Lane. There's supposed to be the ghost of a lady haunting upstairs and a man in the corner seat. Apparently he died in an accident after leaving the pub one night'.

*Prior's Court*

In 1988 a stockman at Prior's Court, Staplow, saw the ghost of a woman by the brook, a tributary of the River Leadon. Mr. Jack Parry, who farmed for many years at Prior's Court, and died in 2002, put into verse the story of how an insanely possessive miller murdered his daughter's lover:

> So nightly now she searches still
> In the murky waters round the mill
> To find her lover as of yore
> And woo him as she did before.
> She rakes the waters to and fro
> And searches for him high and low,
> Not knowing that her father lied,
> Or how her lover really died.
> The lovesick swain she never found
> For in the mill his bones were ground.
> Her father fed him to the swine
> And drank his blood instead of wine.
> So now when dark and bats take flight
> She searches in the dead of night.
> Now should you see her ghostly form,
> Face deathly white and quite forlorn,
> Remember her, this lovesick maid.
> Pass on your way—be not afraid.

## Musical Ghosts

Not all hauntings have such a melancholy origin. A ghostly pianist plays at the sixteenth-century Boot Inn, Orleton. A new landlord, Mr. Roger Broad, took over in 1991. On the first night after opening for business he and his family were awakened by the sound of doors slamming and the piano playing in the lounge. Mr. Broad got up and checked the premises. He found nothing untoward, save for an old, musty smell about the place. He said 'The ghost seems to be friendly. We don't know who it is but we have a theory it may be a former barman here who was painted out of a picture in the bar after an argument with a previous owner'.

Avenbury Church, near Bromyard, is now derelict but it is famous for ghostly organ music which was first heard by a number of people on 8 September 1896. A few years later the vicar himself, Rev. E.H. Archer-Shepherd, heard and described it:

> I was on my lawn and the sound of the music came up from the church quite clearly. It continued all the time I was walking down the meadow to ascertain the cause. When I got within ten yards of the churchyard it ceased. The church door was locked and there was no one within. It was like someone improvising a voluntary on a church organ.

The vicar pointed out that the instrument in the church would have been physically incapable of producing such music, and denied that he had tried to lay the spirit responsible by exorcism. Nevertheless local people tell (or used to tell) this story, which was transcribed by Andrew Haggard:

Avenbury Church? Ah, that's haunted all right. I heered un, I heered the organ a playing and nobody there. Ahd bin to Bromyard to buy a pair of shoes, one Thursday it were, and it were dropping night when I comes to Avenbury. I crossed the stile for the footpath and comes anunt the church and damn me, I hears the organ playing beautiful, and I tell yer, that frit me terrible and I runs all the way to the gate for The Hyde I was that startled.

Well, it come about this way I suppose, There was two brothers lived at Brookhouse, tells me, the one, he were a good chap and a used to play the organ in the church reg'lar. Everybody liked un. T'other he were a sclem [good-for-nothing], never did no work, and was allus a-pothering his brother for money and such. Nobody couldn't suffer un. How it come to happen I don't rightly know, but one evening part they comes to blows on the water bridge over the prill [brook] just off the Bromyard road, and the one he kills his brother for dead. And that weren't the end of it, not by no manner of means for arter that the organ used to play nights and no lights nor nobody there. A could hear un on the road and all quiet— there's scores heered un one time or another.

That come to be the talk of the place, and presently that come on so powerful the passon he say he must fall the ghost, so one day at the same time as the murdering he comes to the bridge all in his clothes and he lights three candles and he starts to pray and presently the one candle that flickered and went out. The passon he prays harder but it warn't no good for the second candle that went out too. Then the passon he prays that hard till the sweat fair run off his nose, and the third candle that started to go down but the passon kep on a

*Avenbury Church*

praying and just when it burned blue it come up bright again, and just so well it did as if it had a gone out the ghost would ha' bested un.

That didn't stop the music altogether but the pain had gone out of it and them as lived about there didn't take a lot of notice, but strangers as knowed about it wouldn't go near or nighst the place arter dark, and them as didn't know, well, they got tarrified.

Ah, I knowed the church well daytimes, my wife's brother was married there and it were there I stood [became godfather] for the daughter of Milly Preece as were cousin of my mother's, but after that Thursday I never went nigh the place again, nights, nor I wouldn't now, neither.

Perhaps the ceremony of exorcism denied by Rev. Archer-Shepherd was an ancestral memory of the one carried out for an earlier ghost at Avenbury, that of Nicholas Vaughan who in the Middle Ages burnt down a palace belonging to the bishop of Hereford. Twelve priests with twelve candles successively read the unquiet spirit into a silver casket which was buried beneath a stone in the River Frome, close by the church. Sceptics suggested that the story was put about to conceal the hiding of plate on the suppression of the monastery which once stood on the site of Avenbury's vicarage meadow.

Churches, churchyards and parsonages certainly seem to have their share of ghosts. Hereford was once 'in a great flutter' about the ghost of a mysterious Mr. Hoskins which was haunting the cathedral at about the time (1786) when the west wall collapsed. Twelve parsons went in, each with Bible, prayer book and candle, and stood in a circle. As midnight struck one of them summoned Mr. Hoskins, who first said he was in Ireland, then appeared. He asked to be laid in the Red Sea, but the parsons decided that he should be under running water, and chose the Bye Street Gate bridge (near the present Kerry Arms). When the ceremony was over only one candle remained alight. Canon Underwood's servant girl later said that his shirt was wringing with sweat when he got home. Years later when the Bye Street Gate was being pulled down an eye-witness heard one of the workmen say 'they hoped they would not disturb Hoskins' ghost'.

St. Peter's Church at Hereford had a cowled figure which two policemen saw one Christmas—in 1926—walking through stout iron gates and an oaken door. News of the incident prompted the son of a former organist at the church to tell how his father had always found 'something uncanny' about the place during the month of December, and avoided being there alone. On several occasions he had seen a robed figure which vanished through doors or into thin air. One explanation for the apparition connected it with the murder of a monk at the altar by marauding Welshmen; another with the death of Walter de Lacy who fell from the tower of the church he built for the monks in the thirteenth century.

The same cowled figure—or another like it—started to appear eight years later in the cathedral close, and was again initially encountered by policemen. Further sightings followed, and something of a vogue for ghost spotting arose, with up to 200 people congregating on the green—'like going to a football match', said one—by the cathedral in the early hours of the morning. Local residents complained. The cathedral authorities alleged that a practical joker was responsible for the apparitions. The watchers gradually thinned out but the cowled and cassocked monk continued to be sighted from time to time. The story is perhaps not ended, for he may be seen again.

A final story concerns the composer, E.J. 'Jack' Moeran, who lived at Gravel Hill, Kington, for a number of years, and often stayed at the rectory in Ledbury with his brother (incumbent 1945-50) and his mother, Esther. He died

*E.J. Moeran*

in Ireland on 1 December 1950. At about 4 p.m. on that day a Ledbury woman who knew the Moeran family very well spotted the composer, as she thought, in the High Street. Knowing that he had been away, and glad to see Jack back in town she made as if to cross over to talk to him, but desisted when he made the familiar gesture of holding up his hand as if to stop the traffic which he normally used if anyone should try to speak when he was listening to music on the radio. The woman turned away, offended. As soon as she saw Esther, his mother, she began to complain only to discover that at the time and day in question Jack's dead body was being brought ashore from the waters of the Kenmare River into which he had fallen after his fatal heart attack.

# CHAPTER 7

# Work

Herefordshire is still one of the archetypal green counties. With arable, beef and dairy cattle, sheep, cider apples, perry pears and hops, agriculture remains its principal industry — in spite of enormous changes in technique and, in 2001, the vicious epidemic of foot and mouth disease. It would be entirely appropriate if the projected National Museum of Rural Life at Hereford came to be established, even at the estimated cost of £100 million.

### Farm Work

In spring and summer the working day for farm labourers once ran from six till six, and in winter from first light to dusk. The waggoner (horseman) would start earlier and finish later than the rest since he had his team to look after. He was the top man on the farm, and would deputise for the farmer in his absence. The waggoner was expected to work in all weathers save the absolutely impossible; a drenching downpour was wryly called 'waggoner's rain'. An acre's ploughing was considered a fair day's work, and in accomplishing it with their single-furrow plough the waggoner and his team would walk thirteen miles. Some still do, but only in popular ploughing matches such as the one at Trumpet, near Ledbury.

Such work was a source of immense pride. Bert Morgan of Dorstone looked back to when horses were still the standard motive power on the land:

> There's nothing better than going out ploughing with a team at seven o'clock in the morning with the horses all done up — tail done up, mane done up, brasses shining. It was a wonderful feeling walking behind them, their old ears going backwards and forwards as if they were really enjoying themselves.

Similar sentiments are expressed in *We're All Jolly Fellows*, which was amongst the best known of country songs. This version was sung to Andrew Haggard by Tug Wilson of Canon Frome:

'Twas early one morning at breaking of day,
The cocks was a-crowing, the farmer did say,
'Come, rise my good fellows, come rise with goodwill,
Your horses want summat their bellies to fill'.

When five o'clock comes, boys, we all do arise,
And down to the stable we merrily flies;
A-rubbing and scrubbing, I'll swear and I'll vow
We be jolly good fellows what follows the plough.

When six o'clock comes at breakfast we meet.
Beef, bread and pork, boys, we heartily eat,
And a sliver in our pocket, I'll swear and I'll vow,
We be all jolly fellows what follows the plough.

We gears up our horses and away we do go,
And over our wide lands that sticks just like dough.
The gaffer comes to us, says 'I'll swear and I'll vow
You are all idle fellows what follows the plough'.

I steps up to him and I makes this reply,
'We have each ploughed an acre, you tell a damn' lie;
We have each ploughed an acre, I'll swear and I'll vow
We be all jolly fellows what follows the plough'.

The gaffer he grinned: ''Twas a laugh and a joke.
It's past five o'clock, boys, and time to unhook;
And for your industry I will you regale
With a gallon apiece of the very best ale.

In caring for the horses waggoners employed many traditional cures and recipes. Cobwebs were used to staunch bleeding, and for this reason the chaff-house roof was never swept. The dosages and ingredients for some potions were closely kept secrets. A horse tonic was supplied by dried and powdered oxberry root, otherwise known as black bryony (*Bronica diocia*). Human urine was used to moisten the animal's bait if the appetite needed stimulating. Tobacco rubbed each day on his bit kept him free of worms, and a pinch of blue vitriol (copper sulphate) made him lively enough to 'jump through his collar'.

Horses' names were chosen from a select, traditional list. The most popular were: Bert, Blackbird, Bonny, Bounce, Bowler, Boxer, Brandy, Captain, Charlie, Darby, Diamond (always pronounced Diament), Dobbin, Dragon, Duke, Flower, Gilbert, Jerry, Jolly, Lion, Lively, Short, Smiler, Snip, Spanker, Surly and Tommy.

*Farmworkers at Hall Court, Much Marcle, 1896*

Other farmworkers also had their role: the scythemen, for example, who at one time cut all the corn and hay. The scythe had a whole vocabulary of its own, including sned (haft), nibs or tuts (hand-grips), rubber (round sharpening stone) and cayther (hazel or willow wand lashed to the scythe to lay all the stalks parallel).

A team of three or four men would contract to mow for so much an acre. They would work in echelon, the leader—known as the lord—setting the pace. The saying went 'You whet when the lord whets'. A rhyme on scythe sharpening ran:

> Wet it to whet, wet it to whet. The mower be too lazy.
> Give 'im a pint to make 'im work. A quart will make 'im 'azy.

Until the First World War, when wages on the land were 12 shillings a week, labourers had an allowance of cider, usually two quarts a day. The drink was decanted from barrels in the farm cellar each morning and lunchtime into small wooden kegs called costrels by a boy who had to whistle at his task to show that he was not drinking. The men drank from their own cow-horn mugs. In the fields they would always take care to pour a small quantity on the ground as an offering to the gods. A mug would always be passed round in a clockwise direction, 'with the sun', and never against it. Casual labour sometimes received no wages, and was rewarded simply in bread, cheese and cider.

William Watkins, after leaving the army in 1921, was pleased to hear of a casual job mowing with one other man two and a half acres of clover at Gorsley, near Ross-on-Wye, and even more pleased to find cider unlimited: 'When the jar was empty it got filled'. Even better, the farmer paid him 2s. 6d. for the job—a worthwhile sum when the weekly wage stood at £1. (By 1939 it reached 34s.)

The labourer's meals were dawn-bit (breakfast), 'levenses (lunch), fourses (tea) and moon-bit (supper). Most of these were taken afield. Characteristic badges of the labourer were his bait-frail (lunch basket), yorks (thongs tied round the trousers below the knee), white smock and hob-nailed boots.

## Apples and Cider

Many farms made their own cider. Apples were gathered from August to December, depending on variety, of which there are several hundred. Herefordshire favoured Dymock Red, Foxwhelp, Golden Pippin, Hagloe, Leather Coat, Oaken Pin, Styre Apple and Ten Commandments. Kingston Black and Redstreak were also popular, and many exotic-sounding varieties inclued Brown Snout and Slack-ma-girdle—both still in production.

*Apples being tumped in a Herefordshire orchard in 1908*

*Portable cider press at Bartestree*

John Philips died in Hereford in 1709 and is commemorated in the cathedral. His epic-style poem, *Cyder*, celebrates the beverage at great length, mentions many varieties of apple, and gives pride of place to the Redstreak:

> Hail *Herefordian Plant*, that does disdain
> All other Fields! Heav'n's sweetest Blessing hail!
> Be thou the copious Matter of my Song,
> And Thy choice *Nectar*; on which always waits
> Laughter and Sport, and care-beguiling Wit,
> and Friendship, chief Delight of Human Life.

At picking time—anything from September to December, depending on the variety—those apples which had not fallen to the ground were shaken or knocked down—the local word was pothered or panked—with long ash poles. Women picked up the fruit and put it into sacks to be taken to the press. There are still some 2,000 stone mills in Herefordshire alone, but now largely ornamental, their use long superseded by the scratter or scratcher mill driven by a small but noisy engine. The pomace (pulp) so produced was put between hairs (coconut matting; originally horsehair) and pressed.

The juice—at first muddy brown, then golden—was put into hogsheads to ferment. Some preferred if possible to add blood, beef, bacon or rabbit skins— all useful for adding nitrogen to feed the yeasts in the fermenting juice—but,

*Cider mill still in use in Herefordshire in the 1950s*

contrary to popular belief, not rats. There is a story of a prize pig which disappeared during cider making one year. Twelve months later when a four-hundred gallon vat was cleaned out its complete skeleton was found. 'Best drop of cider we ever tasted', said the farmer.

Many believed that cider-making should be done only when the moon was on the wane, otherwise the cider would turn sour. When it did become too acid it was known as 'belly vengeance'. Perry at the best of times was said to 'go round like thunder and out like lightning'.

Daniel Defoe was agreeably surprised to find in early eighteenth-century Herefordshire 'that several times for 20 miles together, we could get no beer or ale in their public houses, only cider; and that so very good, so fine, and so cheap, that we never found fault with the exchange'. Others deplored what they thought to be excessive consumption of cider.

Two hundred years after Defoe's time, the Royal Commission on Licensing of 1929-30 declined to recommend an extension in the opening times of public houses. Among those giving evidence was Dr. Weekes, the bishop of Hereford, who expressed the view that 'There is a great deal of secret cider-drinking in Herefordshire'. His reported remark caught the eye of Edmund Knox (1881-1971), who wrote for *Punch* under the pseudonym of Evoe. From 1932 until the 1950s he was the magazine's editor, and from an even earlier period he rented a cottage at Knill, near Kington, so he knew the area well. His poem, *Hell in Herefordshire*, appeared in *Punch* on 18 June 1930:

*E.V. Knox ('Evoe')*

The wild white rose is cankered
Along the Vale of Lugg,
There's poison in the tankard,
There's murder in the mug;
Through all the pleasant valleys
Where stand the pale-faced kine
Men raise the Devil's chalice
And drink his bitter wine.

Unpseakable carouses
That shame the summer sky
Take place in little houses
That look towards the Wye;
And near the Radnor border
And the dark hill of Wales
Beelzebub is warder
And sorcery prevails.

For spite of church or chapel,
Ungodly folk there be
Who pluck the cider apple
From the cider apple tree,
And squeeze it in their presses
Until the juice runs out,
At various addresses
That no one knows about.

139

And, maddened by the orgies,
Of that unholy brew
They slit each other's gorges
From one a.m. till two,
Till Ledbury is a shambles
And in the dirt and mud
Where Leominster sits and gambles
The dice are stained with blood!

But still, if strength suffices
Before my day is done,
I'll go and share the vices
Of Clungunford and Clun,
But watch the red sun sinking
Across the march again
And join the secret drinking
Of outlaws at Presteign.

The poem was widely admired. A sung version, with place names suitably changed, turned up in Worcestershire in the 1980s. A decade later Michael Raven published a musical setting of the original words in his book, *The Land of Lost Content.*

Despite such warnings, in the last decade of the twentieth century there was a tremendous revival in cider making and drinking. Old-established firms like Bulmers and Westons have been joined by Dunkertons (founded in 1981) and many small enterprises, some of which have featured in the Big Apple festivals organised since 1989 in the villages of Aylton, Preston, Putley, Much Marcle and Yatton.

The establishment of a national Apple Day on 21 October has led to many celebrations, including dancing by morris sides such as Ewyas Harold's Foxwhelp, which takes its name from a cider apple. Leominster morris men, who also perform on Apple Day, have been closely involved in reviving the ancient tradition of wassailing orchards in winter (see chapter 10), which underlines the reverence in which apple trees were once held.

## Hops and Beer

'A certain care but an uncertain profit' was one Herefordshire saying about hop growing. Another observed that 'if it were not for the hops the farmers would have to hop themselves'. 'A hop picking morning' meant fine weather in late August or early September, with mists and dews followed by sunshine and sharp air.

For many generations—until the 1960s—picking was done almost entirely by hand. Local labour was supplemented by workers—mainly women, accompanied by their children—brought in from Birmingham, the Black Country and South Wales. Kathleen Dayus (born in 1903) remembers being brought all the way from Birmingham by horse and wagon but most travelled on special trains arranged by the farmers. George Dunn (1887-1975) recalled:

> When th' 'op pickin' season come, about the beginin' o' September or the latter end of August we'd sometimes be away for six weeks. The train was 'ired an' if you were 'ired you 'ad a ticket of th' agent. That was

*Hop picking (Alfred Watkins)*

*Mrs. Eva Priday (seated, left), with family members and others at Trumpet, near Ledbury, c.1952*

> goin' from Cradley {Heath} to Worcester, an' went on to Leigh Court an' Tenbury an' Knightwick, Suckley, Leigh Sinton, Bromyard, Pershore. There's not many I 'aven't bin to. I used to love the 'op fields. We stayed in the barns, all the stables an' cowsheds an' that, just accordin' to the amount o' pickers they wanted. The animals were taken out and the stables white-washed and plenty o' new straw put in.

The work was exacting, pay (by the bushel) modest and conditions spartan, but there was a tremendous camaraderie among the pickers, and plenty of singing:

> Lovely in th' 'opyard. Everybody was a-singin'. You sung while you were pullin' the 'ops off. We 'ad sing-songs round the fire. I've 'ad some good times down the' 'opyards. I 'ardly missed a year. It was the best o' my days.

The sentiments were echoed by many thousands of other pickers. Both farmers and workers cherish memories of the old hop picking days. Mr. Jack Parry, ran at Prior's Court, Staplow, one of the biggest hop farms in the west of England. His pickers came from Dudley in the Black Country, Abertillery in Wales, or were gypsies. When a gypsy king known as Black Harry died at Prior's Court his magnificent caravan was ritually burned. On a different occasion a fire and brimstone preacher who came to harangue the Welsh was run out of the place

*Cribbing, after an engraving of c.1780*

with clear sexual overtones. The women would sometimes band together to retaliate by up-ending the binman or busheller into a crib and covering him with bines. In earlier times a woman would be thrown in with him too, thus enacting a kind of fertility rite meant to ensure a good harvest the following year.

*Procession led by measurer carries last hop pole back to farm
at Much Marcle, 1912*

Mrs. Leather reports another ritual:

> At the conclusion of the hop picking ... it was formerly the custom to
> choose a King and Queen of the Hop-pickers. The head pole-puller, gaily
> bedecked with ribbons and sprays of hops, walked in front of the last load
> of hops from the hop-yard. Behind this came the two hop-pickers, who
> were chosen to be King and Queen; the woman wore male clothing, and
> the man a woman's dress. They, like the pole-puller, were adorned with
> hops and streams of coloured paper; all three carried poles of hops deco-
> rated in a similar fashion, the finest poles being reserved for the purpose.
> This procession went from the hopyard to the homestead, followed by all
> the other hop-pickers and labourers, singing and making merry. The King,
> Queen, and pole-puller removed their decorations at the barn door, while
> the poles they carried adorned the barn or granary until after the ball,
> which usually took place the same evening. Afterwards the hops would be
> carefully dried and hung in the farmhouse kitchen.

A pale echo of such vivid ceremonies is the practice still followed of
displaying hop bines at harvest festivals or using them to decorate rooms in
public houses. The Boot Inn at Orleton holds a barbecue and blessing each
October to mark the successful completion of the hop harvest and to look
forward to the next.

*Lower Venn Farm, near Bromyard: machine-stripping hops from bines, 1998*

## Farm Wisdom and Custom

'Live as though you were going to die tomorrow; farm as though you were going to live forever', so runs a wise Herefordshire saying. A great deal of lore was transmitted in the form of memorable axioms and rhymes. Of the poplar it was claimed:

> Cut me green and keep me dry,
> And I will oak or elm defy.

The birch had similar properties:

> Heart of oak is still and stout;
> Birch says, If you keep me dry I'll see it out.

On the subject of oaks, people believed that 'the man who plants oaks, like the man who plants pears, plants for his heirs'. Alternatively:

> Who sets an apple tree may live to see its end.
> Who sets a pear may set it for a friend.

For planting acorns, nuts, cherry or other fruit stones to grow into trees the best time is from the fall of the leaf until Christmas. For crops of grain the conventional advice used to be four seeds in each hole:

> One for the rook, one for the crow,
> One to rot and one to grow,

Wheat should be sown in the dirt (moist soil), and rye in the dust. Farmers expected to complete sowing wheat by Allontide or Allhallows (1 November). If they had finished by the previous night a cake was divided between the dairy-maid and the waggoner. However if the latter could succeed in getting into the kitchen by a certain hour at night, and cracking his whip three times, the cake belonged to him; but if the dairymaid, by any means in her power, could prevent this she could claim half the cake. She would be on the lookout well before the appointed time, and the duel of wits between the two parties afforded much amusement to the spectators.

In earlier times, though, the aim was that 'At Michaelmas Fair [29 September] the wheat should hide a hare'. All seeds were set as the moon waxed, roots as it waned. Pigs were killed at the moon's waxing, otherwise—it was believed—the bacon would waste away with the moon. (At Eastnor—and no doubt in other parts of Herefordshire—the date for a cow to calve was thought to be retarded or hastened according to the waxing or waning of the moon.) Every pig has four small holes in the skin inside the front ankle, and it was believed that this showed where Old Nick entered the Gadarene swine. Conversely, the black cross on the back of every donkey is a reminder of Christ's journey to Jerusalem.

A donkey was kept with cows in the belief that it would ensure that they never aborted. In the days when farmers took a lantern to visit their cowsheds at night it was considered that on no account should they put it on the table when returning to the house or a cow would lose her calf. At Ledbury a cow was not named until after having her first calf. That is perhaps why vague appelations such as Fillpail were once used. (Some of these figure in wassail songs).

A horse found unaccountably sweating in the stable, first thing in the morning, was believed to have been ridden overnight by witches or fairies. This could be prevented by nailing over the door a cross made of mountain ash or birch. For a horse to have three white feet was very unlucky; hence the rhyme, 'One buy, two try, three don't go nigh'; and also:

> One white foot, buy him;
> Two white feet, try him.
> Three white feet, doubt him;
> Four white feet, do without him.

On the other hand, according to a Herefordshire maxim, 'a good horse is never a bad colour'. As to the animal's treatment:

Up the hill press me not;
Down the hill trot me not.
On the level spare me not;
In a stable forget me not.

In Herefordshire until late in the nineteenth century the custom was kept of bleeding horses on St. Stephen's Day. The occasion was sacred in Scandinavia to the goddess, Freya, and horse races were held in her honour.

It was thought unlucky to keep sheep in the same field for two Sundays running, so before they heard the church bells on the second Sunday they should be moved to fresh pasture. When any animal was sold a little of the purchase price was returned by the seller to the buyer as luck money, a custom still widely followed, and even extended to motor vehicles.

Corn was once measured by the bushel, the size of which varied from place to place. A bushel measure for hops has been preserved in the church in Bromyard. The tod (28 pounds) was employed for wool. In hedging and ditching until relatively recently the rod, pole or perch (five and a half yards) and the chain (22 yards) were used. The latter still applies to cricket pitches, but very little else.

Farm tenancies ran from Candlemas (2 February) or Lady Day (25 March), and the latter is still the date on which many farm rents fall due. A tenant destined to move into a farm at Candlemas had the right of access to plough land from the previous 1 November, together with stabling for two horses and a room for a ploughman. Similarly, a tenant leaving at Candlemas could keep his cattle on the pasture and retain the use of the house and some of the build-ings until 1 May. It was customary when a young couple took possession of their first tenancy for neighbouring farmers to help them establish themselves during the first season.

A number of calendar customs were kept on farms. One ancient tradition enjoyed its first celebration of a new millennium in January 2001 when a plough was blessed during a service held in St. Mary's Church at Humber, near Leominster. Four parishes—Docklow, Hatfield, Pudleston and Stoke Prior—joined Humber to decorate the church to represent the four seasons. Local people hoped that the blessing, revived only the previous year, would become an annual fixture close to what was the start of the agricultural year, the Monday after epiphany (Twelfth Night).

On Easter Sunday there was a ceremony called corn showing, when the bailiff, the men and their families went into a wheat field with supplies of plum cake and cider. They ate and drank in the field, then marched across it with joined hands, saying:

Every step a reap, every reap a sheaf,
And God send the master a good harvest.

A small piece of cake was buried in a corner, with a drop of cider poured on top. A similar procedure was followed in orchards. In the wheat fields, according to Fosbroke, the ceremony originated as a mass weeding of the crop to ensure that no corn cockle (*Agrostemma githago*) were present, since if its seeds were ground with the corn and got into the bread, anyone eating it would suffer from dizziness. The best weeder was allowed to claim a kiss from the prettiest maid, together with the biggest piece of cake at the feast.

Farmworkers, both male and female, indoor and out, were hired on an annual basis at 'mop' fairs held in May or October. Bromyard's was on 3 May, with a second on Whit Monday—'the greatest fair of the year'. Pembridge and Weobley also favoured May, before haymaking, but Ledbury preferred October, after harvest. Of the latter, John Masefield wrote enthusiastically:

> On that great day in October there was a joyous holiday. It was a hiring fair, where men sought employment for the coming year, and the broad main street was glad with the sports of the fair: swings, merry-go-rounds, and coconut shies. It was also busy with the work of the fair: the sale of beasts of many kinds, which came there looking their smartest to be judged and tried, in pens in the crowded street in the tumult of noise that made the fair so wonderful. ... As it was a hiring fair, one saw the country crafts offering their skills: the shepherds, carters or cattlemen, and many indoor and outdoor workers who sought new masters for the coming year.

The mops at Bromyard and Ledbury are still held, despite much grumbling by shopkeepers in the latter town especially, who claim that it kills their trade.

In the past mops were bitterly attacked by police and clergy. A rare defence, urging reform rather than abolition, came in a pamphlet, *Old Mops Mended, Not Thrown Away*, published anonymously but possibly written by Rev. William Poole of Hoarwithy. By contrast, another parson, Rev. E. Jackson, Herefordshire's inspector of schools, wrote in 1860:

> When the *business* of day has drawn to a close, the *pleasures* of the evening commence. The inexperienced lad and lass, with the fruits of their last year's labour in their pockets, are naturally led for refreshment to the neighbouring public-house. ... To the stupefying effects of tobacco are added the intoxicating consequences of deleterious beer and spirits, and the maddening results of dancing and music. Each female selects her male companion for the evening, whose duty it is to see her to her distant home at the close of the amusements in the darkness of the night. Decency forbids me from entering into further details, and I cannot picture to you the proceedings of the night to its close. The very devils in hell would delight and be satisfied with the orgies and revels that follow.

At Hay-on-Wye, just over the Welsh border, hirings continued until the Second World War. Both farmers and farmworkers from West Herefordshire attended, and many still have recollections. One Dorstone farmer remembers hiring a young Welsh lad who lasted only a few days before homesickness proved too strong for him.

At the hirings workers wore an emblem of their calling: some wool in the hat for a shepherd, a piece of plaited straw or even a miniature corn dolly for a waggoner, a few strands from a mop for a housemaid (and hence one explanation for the name of the event). At one time 'each man had to carry his clean Sunday smock on his arm, to show he possessed one, or no good master would engage him'. When a bargain was struck the farmer would give a shilling, known as earnest money, to seal it. Normally, both sides would respect it. A waggoner at Ross-on-Wye was told 'If your character is satisfactory you can start work on Monday morning'. Next day the farmer received a postcard with the laconic message 'I a yeard on yer, and I bent a-coming'.

Harvest was—as it still is—the climax of the farming year. The last few stalks of the last field were called the mare. The reapers tried to cut this by throwing their hooks or sickles at it. The one who succeeded had the mare, and either plaited it himself or gave it to the mistress of the farm to do so. The plait would be hung with the bush burned in the early hours of New Year's Day (see chapter 10) in the farm kitchen to bring luck. Other corn dollies were fastened to the thatch of ricks or used to adorn harvest suppers or harvest festivals in church. The art of making them dates back to mediaeval times, and is still widely practised. The dollies, which symbolised the harvest spirit, were carefully kept through the winter and ploughed in during the following spring.

The arrival in the stackyard of the last load of sheaves was greeted with due ceremony. Then followed a harvest supper given by the farmer to his workers and their families in the great kitchen or even a barn spruced up for the occasion. A liberal meal would be followed by a bout of drinking, dancing and singing until anything up to six o'clock the next morning. In Herefordshire the custom was for the main dish at the meal to be goose.

The famer's health would be drunk, with toasts such as this:

> Good health to the master and all on his farm;
> May he live long and prosper and grow good croos of corn,
> Wheat, oats, beans and barley, and all kinds of grain,
> So that he may have plenty to to treat us again.

The church harvest festivals which succeeded harvest homes were extremely sedate in comparison, but some of the old vigour lingered in places. Until the 1920s the harvest festival celebrations at Sutton St. Nicholas were seen as the main event of the year:

*Harvest Home from Chambers's* Book of Days *(1864)*

The service was always held at three o'clock on a Friday afternoon in early October. All the local farmers attended and all the workmen were given the afternoon off. The church and porch were beautfully decorated, with huge sheaves of corn, and every householder sent their offerings of fruit, vegetables and flowers. A huge tea was prepared in the school and all the villagers were welcome. A dance followed, with the lancers, gay gordons, military two-step and the polka. The men were warned not to swing the ladies off their feet in the lancers but of course they did. Often their shoes fell off and there was a great scramble to return them afterwards. Some of the local comics did a turn in the festival—often hilarious.

Something very similar took place at Eardisland, and no doubt eslewhere. Harvest suppers continue in many villages but they now tend to be a kind of

*Harvest Home*

community celebration organised by volunteers, with participants paying their own way.

After the corn had been carried from the fields gleaners were normally allowed into the stubble to pick up any loose ears for their poultry. 'Though the new binders swept the cornfields clean', wrote John Masefield in 1943, 'the farmers still gave gleaners leave to glean'. Some farmers moved their own poultry houses into the fields so that their hens could glean for themselves. Some fields might be left with their covering of loose ears to attract game and sticks might be scattered to snag the nets of poachers before the local estate agent could organise shooting parties. 'The full moon used to see many people out into mischief', says Mr. Stanley Yapp.

There was also once a kind of gleaning from orchards, called griggling. An anonymous Herefordshire contributor to Hone's *Every-day Book* wrote in 1826:

Leasing in the corn-fields after the sheaves are borne to the garner, is performed by villagers of all ages, that are justly entitled to glean, like ants, the little store against a rainy day. But after the orchard is cleared, ... the village ... climbing boys collect in a posse, and with poles and bags, go into the orchard, and commence *griggling*.

The small apples are called *griggles*. These, the farmers leave pretty abundantly on the trees, with an understanding that the urchins will have mercy on the boughs, which, if left entirely bare, would suffer. Suspended like monkeys, the best climbers are the ring-leaders; and less boys pick up and point out where an apple still remains. After the trees are cleared, a loud huzza crowns the exertion ... Then the hostess, or her daughter, brings a large jug of cider and a slice of bread and cheese, or twopence, to the great pleasure of the laughing recipients of such bounty.

Another climactic occasion was New Year's Day. Some farms roasted their finest ox to be eaten by their workers on 1 January. In parts of Herefordshire it was customary for farmworkers to go on strike. Anyone failing to join in was forcibly carried on a ladder to the nearest public house, and released only on putting sixpence into the drink kitty. Few people in any case can have been fit for work on New Year's Day after the bush-burning celebrations of the early morning.

Twelfth Night, too, played an important part in the rituals of the farming year, and this is described in chapter 10. The Monday following—Plough Monday (see above)—marked the beginning of another cycle of activity for all those who worked on the land.

# CHAPTER 8

# Songs

Herefordshire has a long and rich history of music. Singing and playing instruments were part of the pattern of life for ordinary people, both on special occasions such as harvest suppers or family gatherings, and during the daily round of work. There is considerable evidence of music in mediaeval times, sometimes frowned on by the church; and in more recent centuries ballads circulated, both in print and orally, on a wide range of topics: love and marriage, crime and punishment, sport and entertainment, politics and religion. The place of such songs now seems more in schools and folk clubs than the community at large, but many people continue to sing and enjoy them.

## Monks and Minstrels

One of the earliest and most celebrated English songs, *Sumer is icumen in*, may well have been composed in Leominster Priory by William of Winchester, a monk rusticated there from Reading in the 1270s for sexual misbehaviour. In 1281, charged again with 'incontinence' with various women, he failed to answer a summons to appear before Bishop Cantilupe at Hereford, and was summarily excommunicated.

He then vanishes from the record, though his song remains. Ironically, its pastoral text can be read as vaunting not spring but sex, with the cuckoo alluding to a cuckolded husbancd. The alternative Latin words written below the English are a religious song beginning *Perspice Christicola*, but evidently they failed to save the author from disgrace.

A different musician, a harper called Philip, had a happier experience with Bishop Cantilupe. Five years after the latter's death, many miracles are said to have occurred when in April 1287 his tomb was moved to the north transept of Hereford Cathedral. Among the earliest of these was claimed to be the curing of Philip's lameness.

A couple of decades later—in 1306, to be precise—the first reference in the Hereford accounts to a payment to musicians, two of the earl of Hereford's

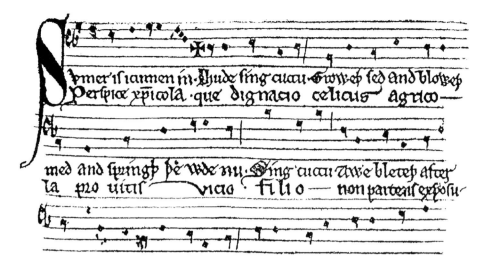

*Part of the manuscript of* Sumer is icumen in

trumpeters. These are presumed to have been acting as town waits, civic musicians paid to play at various official events. By the late sixteenth century the Hereford waits were proficient enough to be hired out by magnates such as the Scudamores and by other towns such as Leominster. In addition they were engaged to play by craft guilds such as that of the Hereford Barbers.

Other—freelance and unofficial—musicians, were called minstrels. During the late sixteenth and early seventeenth centuries their names often appear in the records, kept in a mixture of Latin and English, of the consistory courts which sat in Hereford Cathedral and sometimes in parish churches to adjudicate on religious offences. The punishment given was often penance (after confession) but could be excommunication. Playing instruments on Sundays, especially during the time of church services, frequently caused minstrels to be summoned.

For example, Thomas Davy ap [son of] Bevan was in trouble at Bromyard for piping in service time and fetching a summer pole (Maypole) from Avenbury. Thomes Waties played for dancers during evensong at Leominster in 1595, and in 1611 James Vale of Wellington stood accused of playing and drinking at Bodenham during service time. At Stretton Grandison in 1616 Richard Peres transgressed by playing on the sabbath day and bringing his tabor into church at divine service.

These men are all described as minstrels, which implies that they were professional performers. Other offenders may simply have played instruments in their spare time; those making music in the alehouse at Canon Frome during divine service in 1587 might well have been over-enthusiastic amateurs. The same could be true of William Meney, summoned to appear at Hereford in 1617 because 'he used to plaie one his harpe in the parrish of the haie [Hay-on-Wye] on divers saboath daies in the tyme of evenin praier'. The man failed to appear and suffered excommunication.

A glimpse of an over-keen landlord comes from the Colwall of 1588, when William Poole 'de le black hull' (presumably bull) allowed piping and taboring in his house again in church time. He failed to complete his sentence of ten days' penance, and was suspended from church membership.

Some of the many similar cases from the consistory records are concerned with dancing. They are quoted in chapter 9.

## Ballad Singers

Like minstrels before them, ballad singers sometimes faced prosecution (even persecution) by the authorities. At Hereford before the Civil War a man was sent to the palace prison by the bishop's bailiff for singing and attempting to sell his ballads without leave during St. Ethelbert's Fair.

Three hundred years later one writer, J. Kyrle Fletcher, was asking whether any ballad singers remained in country towns, or whether they had all gone 'in this age of jazz to join the old men who wore smocks and billycock hats, and spoke with the slow, rich speech of the border country'. From his boyhood in Worcester during the 1880s he remembered the singers who came round on market and fair days. He mentions others who 'went to the markets of the three L's: Ledbury, Leominster and Ludlow'.

Some of the very same people might well have been encountered by John Masefield, who writes of Ledbury at much the same period:

> I never crossed the town without the sight
> Of withered children suffering from blight,
> Of women's heads, like skull-bones, under shawls,
> Of drunkards staggering with caterwauls,
> And starving groups in rags, with boots unsoled,
> Blear-eyed, and singing ballads in the cold.

Over 20 years later, in 1908, the composer, Ralph Vaughan Williams, had this experience:

> One evening in Ledbury he heard a girl singing a ballad to two men. The pubs were just closing and these three, standing in the road outside in the light of the still open door, looked like a group in a story.

It is not clear from these accounts whether the ballads at Ledbury were merely sung, or were also for sale in printed form. Kyrle Fletcher leaves no room for doubt in writing about Worcester:

The best remembered of these [performers] was an elderly blind man with a concertina who had a regular stand on the Cornmarket. He was a big stout man with a large white face fringed with grey whiskers. His sightless eyes were closed and he had a perpetual smile, a most unpleasant grin I should better describe it. He was led about by a small boy who carried a number of printed ballads still wet from the printing press, and as the old man sang he moved through the crowd selling the ballads at one penny each. We called this blind ballad singer The Welshman, but anyone who came from west of Malvern Hills was usually called Welsh, even those who spoke with the broad Hereford accent.

From where came these ballads?

## Printed Ballads

Most early street ballads seem to have been printed in London. Some of them make reference to provincial places but have no real connection apart from the mention of a name. *Love Overthrown* from Samuel Pepys' collection looks interesting, but almost any county would do in the compendious sub-title:

> The Young Man's Misery; and the Maid's Ruine: Being a True Relation, How a Beautiful Hereford-shire Damsel (who coming to Live in London, and being greatly Beloved by her Master's Son) was, by her Mistress, Sold to Virginia: and of the Great Lamentation her Disconsolate Lover makes for her.

Other sheets issued in London genuinely dealt with provincial events but are now lost. The titles survive to tantalise, such as *The Miraculous Judgement of God showen in Herefordshire, where a mightie barne filled with Corne was consumed with fure begynninge last Christmas Eeve, and During ffyftene Dayes after* (1595) and *A new Ballad of the late Commotion in Herefordshire occasioned by the Death of Alice Wellington A Recusant.* We do know that the latter refers to an event in 1605 when the vicar of Allensmore refused burial to a catholic woman, and a party of 50 of her co-religionists carried out the interment despite him.

Murder ballads were very much part of the stock-in-trade of the printers concerned, and at least one issued in London but dealing with a local crime has survived. It was printed by the ballad printers, F. Coles, T. Vere, J. Wright and J. Clarke between 1674 and 1679, some 25 years after the events it narrates (and may be a reissue of an earlier sheet which is now lost). Under the title of *The Downfal of William Grismond; Or, A Lamentable Murther by him committed at Lainterdine [Leintwardine], in the County of Hereford, the 12 March, 1650* the ballad is in gothic or black-letter type, adorned with crude woodcuts. Its 22 verses begin:

*Woodcut from* The Downfal of William Grismond

O Come you wilful young-men,
    and hear what I shall tell,
My name is William Grismond,
    at Lainterdine did dwell:
O there I did a murder,
    as it is known full well,
And for mine offence I must dye.

There was a neighbour's daughter
    that lived there hard by,
Whom I had promis'd marriage,
    and with her I did lye,
I did dissemble with her,
    my lust to satisfie,
And for mine offence I must dye.

The unnamed woman becomes pregnant but Grismond knows that because she is poor his well-to-do parents will not agree to their marrying. He murders her and, when the body is found three days later, runs away. He attempts to flee to Ireland but the ship he sails in is 'troubled'—the superstition is as old as Jonah:

> There is some wicked person
> the shipman they did say,
> Within this Ship we know it,
> that cannot pass away:
> We must return to Land here,
> and make no more delay.

Grismond is arrested, imprisoned at Chester, then taken to Hereford to stand trial. The ballad ends as he faces the gallows, warning other young men to take a lesson from his fate. Under various titles it was to live on in Britain and America for over 250 years.

Heavy-handed moralising is also a feature of *Newes from Hereford*, which tells of 'A wonderful and terrible Earthquake' of 1661:

> On *Tuesday* last *October* the first day,
> In *Herefordshire* there happened such a fray,
> By a most terrible Earthquake that did hap,
> And violent storms too by a Thunder-clap.

The conclusion is pointed by a woodcut in which huge forearms issue from stormclouds over the city, one with a sword and the other with a three-thonged whip; between them a trumpet points down, and from it comes a balloon with the single word, 'Repent'. The message recurs in *The Worlds Wonder. Being strange and true news from Leompster in Hereford-shire of one Alice Griffiths, that had four men children at a birth, upon the 25 th. of April last past, 1677.* All four babies died after 25 days of life.

Over a hundred years passed before such ballads were printed in Herefordshire itself. (A 'Popish ballad' mentioned in the Mayor's Court in 1600 in connection with William Cooper, a Hereford bookseller and stationer, has not survived, but was probably printed elsewhere). *A New Song Sung by Members of the Herefordshire Society in London* of 1766 was probably issued there, though T. Davies and Son reprinted it at their Britannia Works in Hereford in 1818.

The Herefordshire Society, founded in London in the time of Charles II, and lasting until the nineteenth century, had 'the Benevolent Purposes of Clothing and Apprenticing ... Poor Children, Natives of the County, or Born of Herefordshire Parents'. At its meetings members sang convivial compositions such as *An Historical Song on Herefordshire* by James Payne. This may be the earliest extant local ballad, first sung in London in 1785 but printed by William Henry Parker at Broad Capuchin Lane, Hereford:

> The Kentish men in partial Lay
> Sing loud in Praise of Kent;

With Marshes, Swamps, and Agues dire,
Poor Souls: if they're content,
So let them be; but I shall make
HEREFORDSHIRE my theme,
And of a finer Garden, sure,
No Poet e'er did dream.

Fruitful its Soil, healthy its air,
For which, as fame doth tell,
King James with Serjeant Hoskins there
For many Days did dwell,
Pleas'd and astonish'd was to see
A Morrice-dance by ten,
Whose ages put together made
A thousand Years - brave Men!

The Fact I've just related
Some Folks will scarce believe;
Stranger things yet there have been,
Or writers us deceive;
For Marcle-Hills did skip and play,
Like Hills in Days of Yore;
Bred on such Soil, no wonder then
Men dancing at five Score.

The County boasts of Wood and Wool,
of Wheat and Women sweet,
Of Hops and Barley, and you can't
Such Cyder elsewhere meet,
Which is made from delicious Fruit,
Such as did Eve beguile;
Her daughters there still drink the juice,
And, like her, love and smile.

Twenty-one more verses follow, equally full of local pride. The many local worthies mentioned include the Man of Ross, the philanthropic John Kyrle, who early in the eighteenth century bestowed on the town as a sort of park some land to the west of the church which became known as the Prospect. This in turn gave rise to a song by one Parry, 'a tradesman in Ross, who afterwards engaged as a soldier, and went to America, where he lost his right arm at the famous battle of Bunker's Hill [1775]. He afterwards returned home, and, with the addition of his pension, supported himself by writing and singing these local and descriptive songs'. So wrote Charles Heath of Monmouth, who published *The Prospect of Ross*, probably in the 1790s, in *The Jovial Farmer's Chest of Conviviality*:

# HEREFORDSHIRE FOLKLORE

Since Poet's soft lays round fair Albion oft ring,
Permit me, although but a shepherd, to sing,
Not of dark solemn groves, nor yet beds of green moss,
But my theme is the delicate Prospect of Ross.

From whence, oh how grateful, appear to the eye,
The serpentine form of the sweet river Wye,
Whose surface unruffl'd displays such a gloss,
As the stream smoothly glides by the Prospect of Ross.

In the sweet month of May, oh what pleasure it yields!
How extensive the view of the meadows and fields!
On the sweet rural banks how the lambs skip and toss,
To please the gay throngs on the Prospect of Ross.

Each summer behold the gay nymphs and the swains,
The shepherds forsake both their flocks and the plains,
Then in haste o'er the fields and the meadows they cross,
To breathe the fresh air on the Prospect of Ross.

At noon to repel Phebus' sultry heat,
How sweet are the elm-rows adjacent retreat,
Where for zephyr's soft breezes they're ne'er at a loss,
Sure no  paradise equals the Prospect of Ross.

*The gateway from the graveyard into the Prospect at Ross*

Let Windsor's soft shades then your lines no more fill,
Your Richmond, nor Kew, nor your Strawberry Hill,
Your Thames rural banks from your books you may cross
And behold them outdone by the Prospect of Ross.

Where Beauty, Health, Wealth, Peace, and Plenty reside,
May Splendor, without Affectation or Pride;
I envy not those their Peruvian dross,
While myself I regale on the Prospect of Ross.

Heath also issued single-sheet ballads, as did a dozen or so fellow small printers in Hereford, Ledbury, Leominster and Ross, mainly between the 1780s and the 1830s. They also did jobbing work such as billheads and leaflets, and supplemented their incomes by selling books and stationery. William Farror of Ross, for example, proudly proclaimed himself 'Printer, Bookseller, Stationer, and Book-binder', and added: 'Genuine Patent Medicines, and Perfumery. Music, Periodical and other Publications procured on the shortest notice. Books Elegantly Bound. Every description of Account Books, ruled and made to Pattern'. Like several other Herefordshire printers, he ran (from 1810) a circulating library. He published two books by Fosbroke, *Ariconensia* (1821) and *Wye Tour* (1826, 3rd ed.).

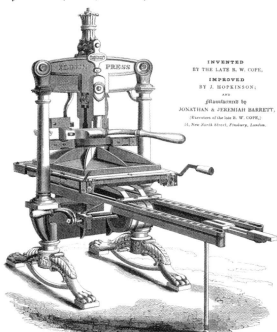

*The Albion Press of 1824, the kind used by many ballad printers*

The output of ballads from these printers—so far as one can tell from what survives, which is probably a mere fraction of the whole—varied from a single example through a handful to several dozen. The most prolific was Thomas Ward of Ledbury, with 53 sheets extant. The total number for the whole of Herefordshire is no more than 200 sheets, but it should be remembered that many of these carried more than one ballad.

Distribution was done through shops used by the itinerant hawkers mentioned earlier. Matthew Child of Eign Street, Hereford, in the 1830s supplied shops at

*Ballad singer at a country wake, c.1733*

Gloucester, Hay-on-Wye, Kington, Leominster and Worcester. As late as 1912 Mrs. Leather wrote of the 'pedlars and ballad chanters, who sang in the streets the ballads they had for sale':

> I have heard of these people often from those who remember them, but could never find one; thye must hve died out. One who came to Weobley Fair every year cried, 'A song, a song, a song for a penny! As large as a barn door and not quite so thick!'

The most plentiful source of material for printers was the stock of their colleagues which they shamelessly appropriated. In this way popular and sentimental songs were reprinted all over the country—*Auld Lang Syne*, *Cherry Ripe*, *Highland Mary*, *Home, Sweet Home*, *Lash'd to the Helm*, *Maid of Llangollen*, *Robin Adair*, and many more. Printers also happily re-issued traditional songs such as *The Baffled Knight*, *The Blind Beggar's Daughter*, *The Cuckoo's Nest*, *The Golden Glove*, *Lord Marlborough* and *The Sheffield Apprentice*.

Printers sometimes achieved apparent local reference by a simple change of name. *Bartholomew Fair* (the first word pronounced Bartlemy) was originally printed in London by Johnny Pitts of Seven Dials. It became *Hereford Fair* when reprinted—without acknowledgement, of course—by T.B. Watkins of Hereford.

Other ballads seem to have been genuinely local productions from the outset. *The Herefordshire Fox Chase* chronicles an epic pursuit:

> All you that love hunting attend to my song,
> I'll beg some indulgence that will be rather long,
> I[t]'s concerning the huntsman, the horse, and the dogs,
> That never fear'd mountains, hedges, ditches, or bogs.
>
> The year 97, Twelfth Eve was the day,
> Bright Phoebus shone clear, and the morning was gay,
> Resolv'd on a chase to which Reynard gave birth,
> I'm sure such a chase was ne'er equal'd on earth.
>
> Squire Percy well mounted, away he did ride,
> James Careless with hounds coupled close by his side,
> Then off to St. Margaret's Park did repair,
> For Reynard long time had been harbouring there.
>
> No sooner arriv'd, as I've since understood,
> But the drag of the Fox they cross'd near the wood,
> Cries James, Hark to Rounder! for that was the hound,
> Which led the whole Pack, and old Reynard first found.

Twenty-two verses and 98 miles later the hunt reaches its conclusion:

> Now Reynard is dead, and my song ends at last.
> Excuse me, I'm thirsty, then push round the glass,
> So I drink with a wish that all great men in place,
> To their king stick as true as these hounds to their chase.

The ballad was printed by T.B. Watkins some time between 1815 and 1836. The author is unknown, but there is evidence that the piece entered oral tradition, though it is not clear whether this preceded or followed its publication by Watkins. A manuscript version of the early nineteenth century—which names the tune used as *Six Bottles More*—has many minor differences of phraseology,

*The music to* Six Bottles More

and spells some places phonetically: dorson (Dorstone), brainton (Breinton) and comb (Cwm), for example. Many years later Noah Richards, a Moorhampton blacksmith, was able to write out the words (albeit reduced to 21 verses) and sing the tune for Mrs. Leather. The powerful exploits of Tom Spring seem to have been left to printers in Birmingham, Bristol, London and even Gateshead (see chapter 2).

## Crime

Locally produced ballads, following in the footsteps of *William Grismond*, did chronicle various crimes. *Elegy on Mary Perry* (1781) laments the murder of a woman by her jealous lover as she was returning from a dance at Leominster to her home at Cholstrey, a short distance away. *The Leominster Tragedy* relates at inordinate length the murder of Mary Cadwallader by her blacksmith husband who was hanged at Hereford in 1816. The sheet, one of the few to acknowledge an author (W. Cartwright), first appeared in Leominster but was evidently thought of enough interest to warrant reprinting in London (by J. Evans and Sons).

*Gritton of Garway*, or *The Murdered Man's Lament*, issued by B. Powle of Ross some time between 1825 and 1851, tells in the first person how an unnamed wrestler goes unwillingly to a contest and meets his death:

> To Garway's cruel Feast I went, it was a hapless night,
> I bring my God to witness I did not wish to fight,
> But Orcop's men are ignorant and savage to degree,
> And nothing else would so but they must have the life from me.
>
> Two seconds they were false and pretended friendship there,
> Oh of such hollow friendship I bid you all beware,
> For long I was a fighting 'till I was out of breath,
> When they held my hands behind me, and I was beat to death.

The dead man is made to argue that such events should be suppressed:

> Oh cruel are these feats indeed, they should be done away,
> And thus to pass in drinking the holy Sabbath day,
> Good gentlemen I pray you, and magistrates be brave,
> And you'll prevent the poor man from sinking to his grave.

A further sheet, *The Death at the Feast*, written probably by Rev. John Webb of Tretire, further emphasises the moralising message. It was printed in London by Catnach, for sale by Seely and Wright of Cheltenham.

Ballad sheets dealing with murders and hangings remained popular in Herefordshire until late in the nineteenth century. Published in 1885, *Double*

*Execution of John Hill and John Williams, convicted of murdering Ann Dickson*, records the first hanging at Hereford to be carried out in private. An engraving shows the gaol with a black flag waving over it. The verses were intended to be sung—incongruously—to the tune of *Ehren on the Rhine*:

> The victim had been labouring,
> In the hop gardens we're told,
> When her work was over then,
> Alas her life was sold,
> She met with Williams & John Hill,
> At a public in the town,
> And before the dawn of early morn,
> In death she was struck down.
>
> (Chorus)
> Side by side they had to die,
> In Hereford goal [*sic*] they both condemned did lie,
> For the cruel Weobley murder,
> For mercy they did cry.
>
> Excited by the drink they had,
> They followed her thro' the field,
> Twas only for a purpose bad,
> To them she would not yield,
> With a little baby in her harms [*sic*],
> No resistance could she give,
> And they gave her wounds while on the ground,
> Till she had ceased to live.

The same format and the same engraving but a different tune—*Just before the Battle, Mother*—were employed three years later for a sheet headed *Execution of Scandreth & Jones At Hereford for the Brutal Murder of Mr. Ballard at Tupley* (Tupsley):

> In the county goal [*sic*] at Hereford,
> Two young men has met their doom,
> No sorrowing friends they had around him,
> There last days past in prison gloom,
> For murder at Hereford they were convicted
> And by the judge condemned to die,
> That sentence now as been inflicted,
> They both in the grave does lie.

(Chorus)
Scandreth and Jones has been executed,
There soul as [*sic*] gone beyond the skies,
They cruelly murdered poor Mr. Ballard,
And on the gallows had to die.

It is unlikely that such ballads were of more than ephemeral interest, but some of the carols printed in the two counties continued to be sung locally for generations afterwards.

**Carols**

In the 1820s and 30s titles such as *The Angel Gabriel*, *The Bosbury Carol*, *Christians Awake*, *A Hymn for Christmas Day*, *Righteous Joseph* and *The Virgin Unspotted* were printed at Hereford, Ledbury or Ross. Early in the following century Mrs. Leather noted that a sheet of carols which included *The Moon Shines Bright* was still being issued at Christmas by a member of the Elliott printing family of Hereford.

With such support from print, many carols entered oral tradition. Tunes were not included on the sheets, so they were passed on by ear, a practice which could lead to strange unions of words and music. In the 1850s some carollers at Marden were heard singing *A Virgin Unspotted* to a tune normally associated with a ballad about Admiral Benbow, *O we sailed to Virginia*. Conversely, a tune sung in Herefordshire to *The Truth sent from above* turns up elsewhere with the words of a drinking song, *Ye Mariners All*.

*The Country Carol Singer, 1869, by Cuthbert Bede*

Mrs. Leather, Ralph Vaughan Williams and Cecil Sharp all took down carols from Herefordshire singers. In December 1907 Vaughan Williams must have been intrigued to receive this letter, especially as the first full text of *The Bitter Withy* had come to light only two years earlier:

> Sir,
> Being 62 years of age, at the age of 10 years I learnt this carol from my mother, in the parish of Yarkhill, Herefordshire.
>> W. Holder
>>> Duke St, Withington, Nr Hereford
> I can sing the Carol in the old Tune but have never saw the Music.

> Our Saviour asked leave of his Mother Mary
>> If he should go to play at Ball
> To play at Ball my own dear son,
>> It is time you was gone and coming home
> But pray do not let me hear of your ill doings
>> At night when you do come home.

> It is up Leencorn and down Leencorn [Lincoln]
>> Our Saviour did he run
> Untill he met with three Jolly Jerdins [young lords]
>> And asked them all three.
> Now which of you all three Jolly Jerdins
>> Will play at Ball with me.

> Oh we are Lords and Ladys sons
>> And born in power all in all [bower and hall]
> And you are nothing but a poor maid's child
>> And born in an Oxen's stall.

> You are safe you are safe you are safe said he
>> You are safe you are safe I plainly do see
> For it is at the latter end I will make it appear
>> That I am above you all.

> So our saviour made a Bridge of the beams of the sun
>> And our [o'er] it went he went he
> And the three Jolly Jerdins followed after he
>> And drowned they were all three.

> So it is up to Leencorn and down Leencorn
>> Their mothers they did hoot & hollow
> O Mary Mary mild call home your Child
>> For ours are drowned all.

So Mary Mary mild called home her child
And laid him across her knee her knee
And she with her hand full of these cold cold bitter withies
She gave him the lashes three.

Oh you cold you cold O you cold bitter Withy
That has made me so bitterley to smart
You shall be the first and the very first tree
That shall perish and die at the heart.

Two years later, Vaughan Williams met Holder at Withington, took down his tune, and later published it in Mrs. Leather's *Folklore of Herefordshire*. One of the other singers the composer met in the same year was the 82-year-old Caroline Bridges of Pembridge, who sang the lugubrious carol, *Awake, Sweet England*, which also appeared in Mrs. Leather's book.

Despite their sombre tone, some traditional carols remained in oral tradition until late in the twentieth century. Two rare survivals were recorded at Christmas, 1978, by Daphne Davies of Bromyard, from Charlie Jones, a retired farm-worker from Castle Frome. One, *How Grand and How Bright* (apparently first printed in Birmingham in the mid-nine-teenth century under the title of *The Worcestershire Carol*), concluded with this verse:

*Mrs. Caroline Bridges of Pembridge (by courtesy of Mrs. Ursula Vaughan Williams)*

And goodwill to man, though his life's but a span,
And his soul all sinful and vile;
Then pray, Christians, pray, and let Christmas Day
Have a tear as well as a smile.

The message was mitigated by a spoken coda:

> I wish you a merry Christmas, a happy New Year,
> A pocket full of money, cellar full of beer,
> A nice fat pig, to last you all the year.
> Apples to roast and nuts to crack,
> And a barrel of cider ready to tap.

*Have You Not Heard* was widely printed in the late eighteenth and early nineteenth centuries, though not in Herefordshire; but singers were not confined to items printed in their own county. Charlie Jones probably learned his version from some other person rather than from a ballad sheet.

Have you not heard of our dear sav-iour's love,___And how he suf-fered like an harm-less dove? And if we in our wick-ed-ness re-main___ Christ will not shed his blood for us a - gain.___

> If we were going to be put to death
> It would be hard to find a friend on earth
> Who would lay down his life to set you free,
> Yet Christ with patience shed his blood for thee.
>
> The sin of drunkenness leave off in time,
> For that's another, a notorious crime.
> Lead sober lives and lay that sin aside,
> Nay, likewise too that odious sin of pride.
>
> Some do by gaining lose their whole estate,
> And then are sorry when it is too late.
> Therefore in time leave off such foolish things
> Which heavy sorrow and destruction bring.
>
> Attend thy church, the sabbath don't neglect;
> The holy scriptures will thy path direct,
> And do no more abuse the name of God,
> Lest he should smite you with his heavy rod.

## THE CELEBRATED CAROL, CALLED
## HAVE YOU NOT HEARD OF
# Our Saviour's Love.
### And another composed by an eminent Writer.

HAVE you not heard of our Saviour's love,
And how he suffer'd like a harmless dove?
But still we in our wickedness remain,
And crucify our blessed Lord again.

If you were going to be put to death
You wou'd find it hard to meet a friend on earth,
That would lay down his life to set you free,
But Christ did shed his precious blood for thee.

Consider what our Lord did undergo,
To prevent them from the gulph of woe;
Repent in time, from wickedness refrain,
Christ will not shed his blood for us again.

Let's love each other as we ought to do,
'Tis God's command, tho' it be kept by few,
For little love does in the world abound,
Nothing but spite and malice to be found.

Yet if we one another do not love,
How shall we think that our great God above,
Will ever take us to his throne on high,
If we each other scorn and vilify.

Here is a thing the Scripture shows
To pray for them that are our greatest foes,
If you think ever for to meet in heaven,
You must forgive, as you expect to be forgiv'n.

'Tis very apt for some to curse and swear,
But let me now persuade you to forbear,
And do not more abuse the name of God,
Lest he should scourge you with his heavy rod.

The sin of drukenness leave off in time,
For that's another sad notorious crime,
Live sober lives, and lay that sin aside,
Nay, likewise the horrid sin of Pride.

Some men make wealth their God, as we do
know
And to their neighbour no charity will show,
'Tis good to help the widow in distress,
Relieve the needy and the fatherless.

Give to the Poor, you lend it to the Lord,
The cheerful giver God doth oft reward,
In that sweet place, where saints and angels
dwell,
How soon your death may come, no tongue can
tell,

Our latter end now let us well consider,
For when our life is gone we know not whither,
Our precious souls may be condemn d to go,
Lord keep us from the burning lake below.

Some men by gaming spend their whole estates
And they are sorry when it is too late,
Therefore in time ward off these foolish things,
Which surely will destruction to you bring.

Keep to the Church, your Sabbath don't
neglect,
The holy Scripture will your soul direct,
Then let it always be your chiefest care,
To spend the Lord's Day in most fervent prayer.

### CAROL II.

### Away dark Thoughts.

AWAY, dark thoughts, awake my joy,
Awake my glory, sing,
Sing songs, to celebrate the birth,
Of Jacob's God and King
Oh, happy night, that brought forth light,
Which makes the blind to see,
The day-spring from on high came down
To cheer and visit thee.

To wakeful shepherds, near their flocks,
Were watchful for the morn,
But better news from heaven is brought,
Our Saviour Christ is born:
In Bethlehem town the infant lies,
Within a place obscure,
Oh, little Bethlehem, poor in walls,
But rich in furniture.

Since heaven is now come down on earth,
Hither the angels fly,
Hark how the heavenly choir doth sing,
Glory to God on High.
The news is spread, the Church is glad,
Simeon o'ercome with joy,
Sings with the infant in his arms,
Now let thy servant die.

Wise men, from far, beheld the star,
Which was their faithful guide,
Until he pointed out the babe,
Whom then they glorify'd.
Do heaven and earth rejoice and sing?
Shall we our Christ deny?
He is for us, and we for him,
Glory to God on high!

Monmouth: Printed and Sold by B. Heath.

ordinary step for a middle-class lady of the time—so as to work alongside gypsy women and first gain their confidence, then hear their songs. She also regularly visited the workhouse at Weobley where to the suppressed fury of the matron she would sweep into her sitting room, take over the piano and gather the old people round it. Among the singers she found there was William Colcombe, who was born in 1827 and learned many of his 30 or so traditional songs from an old nail-maker with whom he had lodged in the village as a youth.

At Pembridge Fair in 1908 Mrs. Leather heard two gypsy fiddlers, John Lock and his brother, possibly Polin. They were two of the nine children of Ezekiel, and were known as the Gentlemen Locks. 'Polin Lock often visited me afterwards', wrote Mrs. Leather in 1926, 'introducing himself by playing away under our windows until we came to listen; but lately I have not seen him, and his wife tells me he is now crippled with rheumatism, and unable to play'. One of the Locks, again possibly Polin, was found dead in the snow near Church Stoke, Montgomeryshire, with his fiddle by his side, and was buried with it.

Mrs. Leather was anxious to share her discoveries and she arranged for Cecil Sharp to meet the Locks at Leominster in 1909. He took down from them several tunes. Sharp returned to Herefordshire in 1921 and during the course of several days spent mainly in the workhouse (later Dean Hill Hospital) at Ross-on-Wye noted some 40 songs from eight men and women whose ages ranged from 64 to 82. (A number of these songs, together with others from Herefordshire, were published by Mchael Raven in 1996 under the title of *The Ross Workhouse Song Book*. A companion CD appeared at the same time).

In 1908 Mrs. Leather met the composer, Ralph Vaughan Williams, at the Three Choirs Festival in Hereford and took him on to meet some of her singers. Vaughan Williams returned in the late summer or autumn—usually hop-picking time—every year from 1909 to 1913 and then again in 1922. During the course of visits to Ashperton, Aylton, Dilwyn, Hardwick, King's Pyon, Madley, Monkland, Monnington, Pembridge, Weobley and Withington he took down some 80 songs, many of them in several different versions. Unfortunately he often neglected the words, but always noted the tunes. One of his excursions—to a hopyard at Monkland—was described by Vaughan Williams as his 'most memorable musical impression for the year 1912' because of the singing of a gypsy. Mrs. Leather's description of the occasion sheds light on her attitude to singers and their songs, and to Vaughan Williams's manner of working:

> After some trouble Dr and Mrs Vaughan Williams and I found their camp in a little round field at dusk, on a fine September evening. There were several caravans, each with its wood fire burning, the Stephens and other families being there, besides Alfred Price Jones, whom we were seeking.

His wife was very ill, and we found him with her under an awning near one of the fires. He agreed to sing, so we all sat down on upturned buckets, kindly provided for us by the gypsies, and while Dr Vaughan Williams noted the tune his wife and I took down alternate lines of the words.

It is difficult to convey to those who have never known it the joy of hearing folk-songs as we heard that pathetic ballad [*Cold Blows the Wind*]; the difference between hearing it there and in a drawing room or concert hall is just that between discovering a wild flower growing in its native habitat and admiring it when transplanted to a botanic garden.

Such was Vaughan Williams' fascination with Alfred Price Jones that he made a special visit to hear him again at Monkland, ten years later. Jones and his wife, Harriet, ended their days in Clun Workhouse.

'Cold blows the wind on my_ true love, And a few_ small drops of

rain.___ I ne - ver had_ but one_ true love; In a green - wood he__was slain.___

'I'd do as much for my true love
As any young girl may.
I'd sit and weep all on his grave
For a twelvemonth and a day'.

When twelve months and a day were gone
This young man he arose:
'Why do you weep down by my grave,
That I can take no repose?

'O fetch me a nut from a dungeon deep
Or water out of a stone,
Or white, white milk from a fair maid's breast,
Or from me begone'.

'How can I fetch a nut from a dungeon deep
Or water out of a stone,
Or white, white milk from a fair maid's breast
When fair maid she is none?

'One kiss, one kiss from your lily-white lips
One kiss from you I crave'.
'The cock does crow and we must part,
I must return to my grave.

# CHAPTER 9

# Dance & Drama

Traditional dance and drama flourished for centuries. The latter, in the form of mumming plays, persists in only a very few revivals but both country and morris dancing continue to thrive. Some claim that morris and mumming are relics of fertility rites whose origins lie in the distant past. This is highly unlikely. The first written reference to morris so far discovered dates from 1448, and to mumming as we know it a couple of hundred years later. The lack of pagan origins does not prevent dancers and actors from providing music and movement, colour and spectacle. In turn, their efforts promote wellbeing, which is surely worthwhile.

## Morris Dance

Whatever its origins, morris was clearly well established in Herefordshire by 1609 when an anonymous but enthusiastic observer wrote: 'Lancashire for Horne-pipes: Worcestershire for Bag-pypes: but Herefordshire for a Morris-dance puts downe not only Kent, but verie near (if one had a line long enough to measure it) three quarters of Christendome'. His pamphlet, *Old Meg of Herefordshire*, describes a performance by 12 dancers whose combined ages totalled over 1,200 years.

A speech introduces the event:

> Ye servants of our mightie king,
> That come from court one hundred mile
> To see our race and sport this spring,
> You are welcome—this is our country stile—
> And much good doe you, we are sorie
> That *Hereford* hath no better for yee.
>     A Horse, a Cocke, Trainsents [drag hound chases], a Bull,
> Primero, Glecke [card games], Hazard, Mumchance [dice games]:
> These sports through time are growne so dull,
> As good to see a Morris dance.

The 12 dancers are carefully listed, and their ages—and sometimes professions—given:

> James Tomkins, gentleman, of Lengerren [Llangarron], the foreman, 106
> John Willis, bonesetter, of Dormington, 97
> Dick Phillips of Middleton, 102
> William Waiton, fisher and fowler, of Marden, 102
> William Mosse, 106
> Thomas Winney of Holmer, 100
> John Lace, tailor, of Madley, 97
> John Carlesse of Homlacie, 96
> William Maio, 'an old Souldier, and now a lusty labourer', of Egelton [?Eggleton], 97
> John Hunt, the Hobby Horse, 97
> John Mando of Cradley, 100
> Meg Goodwin of Erdisland, 120

In addition there were four 'whifflers' or crowd marshals:

*Title page of Old Meg*

Thomas Andros of Beggar Weston [Weston Beggard], 108
Thomas Price of Clodacke [Clodock], 105
William Edwards of Bodenham, 108
John Sanders, ironworker, of Walford, 102

Andros, Price and Winney were subsidy-men, people liable to a pay a subsidy—pecuniary aid granted by Parliament to the king for special needs—and therefore people of means. Both Edwards and Tomkins had small children of six and eight respectively.

Music was provided by two Hereford men, Harrie Rudge (aged 108), who 'tickled a trebble Violin', and Hall, a 'quack-salver' (healer) and 'ex-leach' (97), than whom 'the Wayts of three Metropolitan Cities make not more Musicke than he can with his Pipe and Tabor'.

*Pipe and tabor player and morris dancer*

Of the oldest of the company, Meg Goodwin, we are told that she was Maid Marian to John Mando's Robin Hood, and that she was 'at Prince Arthur's death at Ludlow [in 1502] and had her part in the dole [mourning]; she was threescore years (she saith) a Maide and twenty yeares otherwise'.

The costumes worn were described in this way:

> The Musitians and the twelve dancers had long coates of the old fashion, hie sleeves gathered at the elbows, and hanging sleeves behind: the stuffe, red Buffin {coarse cloth}, stript with white, Girdles with white, stockings white, and redde Roses to their shoes: the one sixe, a white Jews cap, with a Jewell, and a long red Feather: the other, a scarlet Jewes cap, with a Jewell and a white feather: so the Hobbi-horse, and so the Maide-Marrion was attired in colours; the Wiflers had long staves, white and red.

The group's combined efforts, wrote the pamphleteer, were 'as if *Mawlborne* (Malvern) hilles, in the very depth of Winter, when all their heades are covered (in steade of white woollie cappes) with snow, had shooke and daunced at some earth-quake'.

There may have been a degree of exaggeration on the part of the writer, but the event seems to be genuine. Some have placed it at the bottom of the present

Widemarsh Street in Hereford, on open space where horse races took place. Arthur H. Lamont, however, suggests that the dancing was organised by Sergeant Hoskyns at Ingestone House for the entertainment of King James I. If so, it is strange that the pamphleteer did not seize upon the news: his list of notable spectators is headed by Lord Herbert of Raglan, exalted enough, but not in the kingly league.

The presence of a woman dancer, Meg Goodwin (she of the pamphlet's title), would be very unwelcome to some morris purists of today, yet it can be paralleled by a number of instances from the consistory court records (see also previous chapter) of the early seventeenth century.

In 1602 Miles Conney of Tedstone Delamere was arraigned

> ffor prophaininge the Saboathe day and daunsinge and revelinge with morrice dancers tempore divinorum [at the time of divine service], and namely 8⁰ Augusti *ultimo* beinge Sunday, and would not desist albeit he was admonished thereof by mr Grenewiche.

In addition to being required to confess his his wrong-doing and to appear in penitential dress at his church, Conney was required to name his fellow dancers. He listed a large number of men and also women from Tedstone and Avenbury: Thomas Launcie, Thomas Conney, Henry Boyce, William Boulter, Philip Howles, Richard Conney, Tacy Richards, Rebecca Tower, William Morries, Jane Conney, Anthony Conney and James Henge.

Edward Hall, a Ledbury innkeeper, was in similar trouble in 1616:

> hee actor and morrice dauncer, and have gone out of the parrishe to other places, with gune and drume both in the night to the disturbance of the kinges subiettes and the profanation of the Saboath daie in the morning.

Along with Hall were charged Edward Crocker, corviser (shoemaker), Edward Hooper, and John Wilbore, 'ffidler' (also accused of drunkenness and ribaldry).

Three years later, at Yazor, Thomas Hopkins, Thomas Hodges, William Lyke, James Hodges, Anne Lyke, Elizabeth Hint, Margaret Wynne, Anne Watkins and John Watkins, faced charges of 'daunsing the morrice betweene morninge and eveninge prayer on a Sonday and goeinge dauncinge out of that parishe'. The following year at Withington more morris dancers, this time all men faced proceedings, together with Roger Miles, 'for playing on his fiddle'. At Ross in 1629 we are back to a mixed party who danced the morris at the time of 'eveninge praier' during May, June and July: John Machin, James Streete, Thomas Parret, Leticia Vaughan, Jane Cursier, Thomas Browne, Richard Smith, Anna Cater and John Sandy.

After these hectic years, there followed a very lengthy gap in any sort of record of Morris dancing in Herefordshire, until in 1819 an observer from Ross

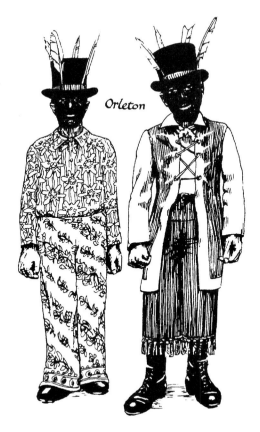

*Orleton*

*Costumes at Orleton*

commented: 'At Whitsuntide, the Morrice-dance is got up in a style worthy even of Mr Douce' (the antiquarian). Two years later Fosbroke wrote that it was 'kept with great spirit'. Then, almost a century later Mrs. Leather observed that 'the only morris dancers I can discover in the country [?county] ... are from Brimfield'. However, between 1800 and 1940 morris was recorded not only at Brimfield but at Bromyard, Cradley, Dilwyn, Elton, Leominster, Orleton, Putley, Richard's Castle, Ross-on-Wye, St. Weonards and Weobley.

At Ross and Walford sides went out at Whitsuntide, much as they did in the Cotswolds; but in most other places where details are recorded—including Brimfield, Dilwyn, Leominster and Orleton—dancers preferred the Christmas period, when they were often short of work and of money. In the border morris—that of Herefordshire, Worcestershire and Shropshire—the characteristic dance is done by multiples of four men, often totalling 12 in all. This is unlike the six a side of the Cotswolds, though the formation described at Hereford in 1609 mentions two groups of six. The dances were vigorous. Short sticks were clashed. The costumes worn ranged from perfunctory to elaborate. For example, at Orleton until the 1920s the performers wore fancy clothes and top hats with feathers. They also blackened their faces. At Dilwyn shirts were profusely decorated with streamers and rosettes, and dancers had pads of bells tied below the knees.

Christmas was not Christmas without the morris, thought many people, but one by one the old sides gave up dancing. However, enthusiasts—usually professional people like the subsidy-men of 1609 rather than hungry workmen—set about a revival, and presented their takings to various charities. The Silurian Morris, founded in 1969 at Ledbury, favours the Border morris dances. Leominster Morris, which celebrates its 20th anniversary in 2003,

*Old Wonder Morris Men at the Ledbury Folk Fair, 1991*

*Leominster Morris on May Day*

performs Border and Cotswold dances in the summer (April to September), Border only in the winter (October to March). During its year of dancing there are three high points: on 7 April (Wordsworth's birthday) at the Wordsworth Stone, near Leysters; on 1 May at dawn at Bache Camp, also near Leysters; and on Twelfth Night at various places in the Leominster area (see chapter 10).

It is interesting to compare the list of members of the Leominster Morris with that of almost four hundred years earlier: Graham Bailey, scientist, 45; Chris Bates, photography lecturer, 39; Ian Elliott, metallurgist, 49; John Gaynor, social worker, 45; Thony Handy, teacher, 51; Dominic Kemp, toolmaker, 37; Tony Locock, gardener, 50; Edmund Locock, schoolboy, 13; Marcus Locock, schoolboy, 13; John Messenger, ecologist, 48; Alan Messenger, student, 17; Allan Pearce, civil engineer, 50; Jim Rann, architect, 44; Trish Sanders, staff nurse, 55; Steve Watters, social worker, 42.

Leominster Morris has a website, has issued a CD recording of a wassailing carried out at Aymestrey in January 2000, and is considering the production of a CD-Rom with music, photographs and also film. Tom Poston, a member of a forerunner to the present side which existed up to 1914, and after whom a stick dance has been named, would no doubt be surprised, but might well accept that technology is being used in the service of tradition.

## Country Dance

For lack of alternative venues, country dancing took place in the open air on village greens, in market places, at crossroads, and even in churchyards. As with morris, consistory court records between roughly 1580 and 1620 have many instances of dancers whose activities offended by clashing with service times. James and Maria Poslons allowed people to dance and minstrels (John

Botchet and John Lewis) to play at their house at Bishops Frome. Thomas Hulland's guests drank and danced at Bosbury. Edward Hopley sold ale and permitted dancing at Dilwyn in 1582. Disorders followed dancing at Eastnor in 1609, and in the same year 'mirth and musique' during Whitsuntide dancing in the churchyard at Goodrich led to fighting which resulted in a case before the redoubtable Star Chamber court.

Dancers fell foul of sabbath restrictions at a range of other places, including Foy, Hentland, Kington, Leominster, Linton, Little Cowarne, Llangarron, Madley, Much Birch, Much Dewchurch, Norton Canon (where playing tennis was added to the charge sheet) and Pembridge (where Ludovic Thomas danced in the church porch). At Putley in 1625 Christopher Jones, Alice Harries, John Lambert, Henry Carpenter and John Boulcott danced every Sunday and holiday 'for the most part' between Easter and Lammas (1 August). Those dancing and playing unlawful games at Ross in 1610 included Thomas Meiricke, junior, a glover, John Taylor, a tapster, and Francis Younge, a weaver.

The catalogue of offending villages continues with St. Weonards, Shobdon, Winforton, Withington and Woolhope (where in 1620 John Powell played the

fiddle for dancing, and those spectating included a clegyman, Anthony Wheeler). Other musicians are mentioned at Pembridge and Leominster, though they must have been present whenever dancing took place, unless sometimes accompaniment came in the form of mouth music.

Yet country dancing survived the church's prosecutions, and became reasonably respectable. In 1993 a slightly macabre reminder came to light at the Portway Hotel, Staunton-on-Wye. During renovation work a green slate casket containing a horse's skull and a green glass bottle with a message inside were found beneath floorboards. The message read:

*English . .*
*Folk Dance*
*Society . .*

*Herefordshire Branch.*

President :
THE LORD BISHOP OF HEREFORD.

FOLK DANCE
FESTIVAL . .
and
COMPETITIONS

. . . . . .

*Herefordshire County Cricket Ground*

*On   Thursday,   June   16th,   1927.*

The Hereford Times Ltd., Printers.

*Programme cover, 1927*

> When this house was rebuilt in 1879, from underneath this floor was taken 40 horses' heads placed there about the year 1800 by order of Sir John Cotterell, Bart., supposed for some musical purpose.

Various theories were put forward to explain the mystery but the solution came from a document indicating that a visitor to the Portway, Thomas Blashill, was told by the landlord in 1852 that two cartloads of horses' skulls were under the floor, 'to make the fiddle go better'. Blashill returned during the refurbishment of 1879 and saw 24 skulls which workmen had found screwed through the eyeholes to the undersides of the floorboards. A similar use of horses' skulls to make a floor more resonant for dancing comes from another Herefordshire inn, where they helped to make a hollow sound when the dancers stamped their feet, 'as was the custom in some old country dances'. I saw the Portway skull in 1993, when the owner decided to display the find in a glass case. However, when I visited again some years later after the place had changed hands the relic was no longer to be seen.

**Mumming**
As with morris there is a long history of popular drama in the county. Until the Reformation lavish and colourful street pageants were mounted by the city craft guilds; in 1503 there were 25 in Hereford alone. The Corpus Christi pageant continued there until the mid-sixteenth century—but was stopped after the accession of Edward VI—and a labourer rode into the city on an ass every year in Passion Week until 1706.

Favourite subjects for the pageants included Biblical themes such as Adam and Eve, Noah, the Annunciation and the Nativity. To some extent they were replaced by plays given by the travelling theatre companies which toured from the time of Henry VIII onwards.

Village drama in the form of mumming plays with a series of knockabout combats is reported from some counties as early as the eighteenth century, but no text came to light in Herefordshire until 1908, when William Powell wrote out for Mrs. Leather the version previously performed at Ross-on-Wye. He said that 'the mumming had been discontinued of late years. He had taken all the parts at different times; the dresses worn were various and fantastic'.

The players at Ross came at Christmas. Their faces were blackened, and they had licence to rush in without knocking at the door. The characters were Father Christmas, St. George, the king of Egypt, Turkey Snipe, Captain Rover, Bonaparte, Little John, Sambo the Minstrel, Prince Valentine, the Doctor, Beelzebub, Farmer Toddy, Head Per Nip and Dicky Hissum.

The Ross-on-Wye text was the only one known from Herefordshire until Dave Jones unearthed others at Cradley and Ledbury some 50 years later. Even references to the play are sparse. In a poem of 1943 John Masefield mentions

*The Leominster Play*

the youthful memory at Ledbury of the 'mummers [who] went at Christmas with their play, with Mrs Vinney who revived the dead' and he refers elsewhere to 'the figure of the St. George of a crew of mummers', this time placing the performance at an October Fair in his native town.

The relative absence, apparently, of the play from Herefordshire remains a mystery. Performances were given in town streets and on village greens, in public houses, farms and (by invitation) mansions. The actors—always male—stood in a line or semi-circle, stepping forward with the formulaic 'In comes I'. Speeches were delivered with due solemnity, punctuated by comic relief and even horseplay, especially where the doctor's part was concerned. The series of stylised combats and deaths, followed by rapid restoration of life, was the essential point of the play. Its text—perhaps one should say texts, for there are many variations, all very similar—might not read very well on the page, but both for actors and audience was (and still can be) very satisfying in performance. No traditional performances survive in Herefordshire, but revivals regularly take place. Leominster Morris (above) does its own composite version, laced with topical allusions, on various occasions, including Twelfth Night.

The Cradley play, of which the text concludes this chapter, was performed by the Old Wonder Morris of Putley for several years, every Boxing Day.

## The Cradley Play

Noted in the 1960s by Dave Jones from Albert Philpotts of Cradley, who knew it as the Cradley Morris Dance. The play was performed throughout Boxing Day at houses and pubs. All the characters were dressed in the same way, their

*The Cradley Play performed at the Butcher's Arms, Woolhope,*
*by Old Wonder Morris*

trousers, jackets and hats being smothered in strips of rag of many colours, the
effect being like that of an old pegged rug. Their faces were blacked. Some
carried instruments—melodeon, tambourine, accordion, mouth organ or
bones—with which to accompany the songs.

Characters

Belzebum, Noble King, Doctor, Raggety Jack, Little Billy Funny.

| | |
|---|---|
| BELZEBUM | In comes, I, Belzebum. |
| | On my shoulder I carry a gun, |
| | In my hand I carry a can. |
| | Don't you think I'm a jolly old man? |
| NOBLE KING | In comes I, the Noble King, |
| | Just arrived from France, |
| | And with my sword and lance |
| | I'll put old Belzebum to a dance. |

*(He hits him with a sword and knocks him down)*

| | |
|---|---|
| DOCTOR | In comes I, the doctor. |
| NOBLE KING | How did you come to be a doctor? |
| DOCTOR | By my travels. |
| NOBLE KING | Where have you travelled? |
| DOCTOR | I've travelled England, Scotland, Ireland and Wales; three times round the world and back again. |
| NOBLE KING | What can you cure? |
| DOCTOR | I can cure the its, the pits, the palsy and gout, Pains within and pains without. If there's nineteen devils in this man I can guarantee to knock twenty out. |
| NOBLE KING | Set about it, then. |
| DOCTOR | In my left-hand coat pocket I carry a box of pills called goosifer lucifer pills. Take one of these, old man. In my right-hand coat pocket I carry a bottle, and this is goosifer lucifer syrup. Take a drop of this, old man, and I guarantee to put you back on your feet again. |

*(Belzebum gets to his feet and they all sing)*

| | |
|---|---|
| ALL *(sing)* | He'll be strolling round the town, Knocking the people down, Tasting every kind of wet, Having a fair you air you bet. Fair-o, fair-o, ricketty, racketty crew. |
| RAGETTY JACK | In comes I, Ragetty Jack, Wife and kids on my back. Two at the Union [workhouse], two at home, Two in the corner chewing the bone. Out of ten I've got these five, And the rest have gone to the workhouse. |
| ALL | Fair enough, fair enough. He's only a local lad. |
| LITTLE BILLY FUNNY | In comes I, little Billy Funny. I'm the one that collects the money. All silver, no brass. Bad money won't pass. |
| ALL *(sing)* | Christmas comes but once a year And it's everyone's delight to keep it up, keep it up. We started going down the town and finished with a fight, When half a dozen of us got run in for the night. |

190

Just the same, boys, yesterday was we,
For the wind do blow and all of the people know
We all got drunk and full of devilment,
We left our darling wives at home and arm in
    arm we went.

Strolling round the town,
Knocking the people down,
Tasting every kind of wet,
Having a fair you air you bet.
Fair-o, fair-o, ricketty, racketty crew.

# CHAPTER 10

# Seasons

Rituals and observances to mark the passing of the year and its seasons have a tenacious hold on people's affections and emotions. Many of those relating to churches and farms have been considered in chapters 3 and 7 respectively; others feature here.

Although they may give the feeling of dating from time immemorial, few rituals have an unbroken history of any length, and some are of recent creation. Several seasonal rituals listed as defunct in 1912 by Mrs. Leather—burning the bush and heaving, for example—were resurrected 60 or 70 years later. Indeed, there seems to be a current fashion, which must respond to a profound emotional need, for reviving calendar customs in particular and folk culture in general. The resumption of events on St. George's Day is a recent example.

Commercial motives may play a part, and also civic pride or the desire to promote tourism. In other cases the joy and satisfaction generated are their own reward. For whatever reason, the celebration of turning points in the year is deeply ingrained, and one can safely predict that in one form or another it is destined to continue.

## January

### New Year's Day

The desire to greet the New Year seems to be increasingly keen, and fireworks have now been widely added to the celebrations. Crowds gather in High Town at Hereford and also in the centres of smaller places such as Ledbury and Ross. These occasions are usually good-humoured, though rowdyism sometimes surfaces, as at Ross in 1991 when policemen were injured and arrests made.

In private houses many still prefer the first caller of the year to be a dark-haired male. Such a person is invited to enter by the front door and leave by the back, contrary to normal superstition which holds that a caller should enter and leave by the same door so as not to take the luck away from a house. The first footers used to greet the occupants with this rhyme:

> Good master and good mistress and everybody here,
> We wish you a merry Christmas and a happy New Year;
> A pocket full of money and a cellar full of beer,
> And a good fat bacon pig for to last all the year.

A male caller was also required both on Christmas Day and the first Monday of the New Year at Ross-on-Wye, or the household would have no luck for a year. Boys were often recruited at the price of a few coppers (pence) to act as first footers. In addition they would go round gifting—asking for a gift or a tip—on New Year's Day.

At Kington in the 1840s boys went 'from house to house with compliments, in the form of a song, at the break of day', wrote Richard Parry. Several decades later, the same sort of thing happened in the villages of the Teme Valley, with one of the singing boys called into the kitchen to receive a reward and to bring luck for the year. In the days of climbing boys who swept chimneys, people booked them for New Year's Day so that they would be sure to have a male visitor, the benefit of whose presence included the traditional good luck of the sweep. (Apparently, since the establishment of the National Lottery, people have taken to touching chimney sweeps in the street again in in effort to achieve fortune).

This account of customs 'observed at Bromyard and its neighbourhood' appeared in *The Antiquary* in 1873:

> As twelve o'clock on the 31st of December, draws near, and the last of the Christmas carols are heard without doors, and a pleasurable excitement is playing on the faces of the family round the Christmas log within, a rush is made to the nearest spring of water, and whoever is fortunate enough to first bring in the 'cream of the well', as it is termed, and who first taste of it, have prospect of good luck through the forthcoming year. Also, in the early hours of the New Year, after a funeral service, as it has been termed, have [*sic*] said over 'Old Tom', as the old year is called at the public houses and ale and cider stores, the streets are filled with boys and men, singing in loudest tones possible:
> I wish you a Merry Christmas and a Happy New Year,
> A pocket full of money and a cellar full of beer,
> And a good fat pig to serve you all the year.
> Ladies and gentlemen sat by the fire,
> Pity poor boys out in the mire.

In parts of Herefordshire there was great competition to be the first to drink water from certain wells or springs after the midnight chimes had announced the New Year. For this practice at Aconbury Well, see chapter 1. At Dinedor the water of the holy well—now no longer in existence, but recorded in the name of Holywell Farm—was especially prized since a drink from the first pailful, 'the cream of the well', was thought to promote health and happiness throughout the year.

Another custom widely observed in Herefordshire was to take down and burn the mistletoe sprig kept twelve months earlier, and to replace it with another, freshly-cut the previous day. Some similarly burned and restored hawthorn. This could be done in the context of a more elaborate ceremony.

At Bredwardine Kilvert made this note in his diary for 31 December 1877 (though it refers in part to the following day):

> I sat up till after midnight to watch the Old Year out and the New Year in. The bells rang at intervals all the evening, tolled just before the turn of the night and the year and then rang a joy peal, and rang on till one o'clock. After I had gone to bed I saw from where I lay a bright blaze sprung up in the fields beyond the river and I knew at once that they were keeping up the old custom of Burning the Bush on New Year's Day in the morning.

The bush was in fact a hollow globe made of twisted hawthorn shoots. In the early hours of New Year's Day it was removed from the farm kitchen where it had been kept for twelve months, filled with straw, fixed on a long pole, and set on fire. Sometimes the burning bush was used to light twelve small bonfires, after which it was consigned to a thirteenth and larger fire. A variant was that one of the men ran with some of the fire on a pitchfork across thirteen ridges of ploughland; if he could keep it alight for all thirteen it was a sign of good luck to come.

Cider was poured on a newly-prepared bush, which was then singed in the fire. The company would chant several times 'Auld ci-der', and then perhaps walk round the fire singing a carol. In liberal measure cider was drunk and cake eaten. The new bush was carefully put in the kitchen to await the following year's ceremony.

*Bush used at Pembridge in 1897, and for some reason saved from the flames*

As early as the 1850s the custom was beginning to die, to the consternation of some people, one of whom (at Kington) told a farmer who was proposing not to burn the bush 'Well then, depend on it, sir, you will have no crop if you do not'. The prediction, sadly in some ways, proved unfounded.

Bush burning did continue in much of Herefordshire until late in the nineteenth century. It survived at a few places near Kington and Leominster until the First World War, or perhaps even later. Then the custom died, or at least went into limbo, but it was revived at Putley by Dave Jones in 1975 and has continued every year since.

## Twelfth Night

Twelfth Night (5 January) and Twelfth Day (6 January) are otherwise known as the Vigil and Feast of the Epiphany. By Act of Parliament the nation changed in 1752 from the Julian to the Gregorian calendar. Eleven days were omitted in the first year, but from then on many country people insisted on sticking to the old dates, at least for certain important occasions. As well as being Twelfth Night, 5 January was therefore Old Christmas Eve.

On Twelfth Night, a ceremony was held which resembled that of burning the bush, and indeed may have been simply a variation on it. As early as 1791 a lengthy description from Herefordshire appeared in the *Gentleman's Magazine*:

> On the eve of Twelfth Day, at the approach of evening, the farmers, their friends, servants, all assemble and near six o'clock all walk together to a field where wheat is growing. The highest part of the ground in always chosen, where twelve small fires and one large one are lighted up. The attendants, headed by the master of the family, pledge the company in old cider, which circulates freely on these occasions. A circle is formed round the large fire, when a general shout and hallooing takes place, which you hear answered from all the villages and fields near; I have myself counted fifty or sixty fires burning at the same time, which are generally placed on some eminence. This being finished, the company all return to the house, where the good housewife and her maids are preparing a good supper, which on this occasion is very plentiful. A large cake is always provided, with a hole in the middle. After supper, the company all attend the bailiff (or head of the oxen) to the wainhouse, where the following particulars are observed: the master, at the head of his friends, fills the cup (generally of strong ale), and stands opposite the first or finest of the oxen (twenty-four of which I hive seen tied up in their stalls together); he then pledges him in a curious toast; the company then follow his example with all the other oxen, addressing each by his name. This being over, the large cake is produced, and is with much ceremony put on the horn of the first ox, through the hole in the cake; he is then tickled to make him toss his head; if he throws the cake behind, it is the mistress's perquisite; if before (in what is termed the boosey), the bailiff claims the prize. This ended, the company all return to the house, the doors of which are in the mean time locked, and not opened till some joyous songs are sung. On entering, a scene of mirth and jollity commences, and reigns thro' the house till a late, or rather an early, hour, the next morning. Cards are introduced and the merry tale goes round. I have often enjoyed the hospitality, friendship, and harmony, I have been witness to on these occasions.

The letter is signed J.W., and a further communication over the same initials in 1820 must be by the same hand because of the many instances of identical phraseology. We learn that Mr. Tully's farm at Huntington (near Kington) is the scene of the activity, and are given a specimen verse of the 'curious toast' to the oxen:

> Here's to thee Benbaw and to thy white horn
> God send thy master a good crop of corn
> Of wheat rye and barley and all sorts of grain
> You eat your oats and I'll drink my beer
> May the Lord send us all a happy new Year.

Versions of the complete song circulated until the twentieth century. Vaughan Williams took this down from a Mr. Dykes at Weobley in 1912:

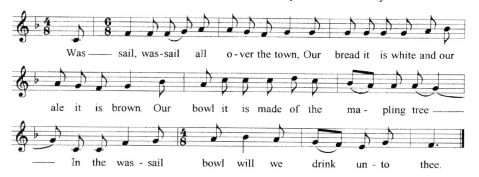

> Here's a health to the ox and to his right eye.
> May God send our master a good Christmas pie,
> A good Christmas pie that may we all see,
> In the wassail bowl will we drink unto thee.
>
> Here's a health to the ox and to his right ear.
> May God send our master a happy New Year.
> A happy New Year that may we all see,
> In the wassail bowl, etc.
>
> Here's a health to the ox and to his right horn.
> May God send our master a good crop of corn.
> A good crop, etc.
>
> Here's a health to the ox and to his right hip.
> May God send our master a jolly fat ship [sheep].
>
> Here's a health to the ox and to his right leg.
> May God send our master a jolly fat hog.
>
> Here's a health to the ox and to his right hoof.
> May God send our master a jolly good crop of fruit.

Here's a health to the ox and to his fat arse.
May God send our master a good crop of grass.

Here's a health to the ox and to his long tail.
May God send our master a jolly wassail.

Come, butler, come fill us a bowl of your best,
And I hope your soul in heaven may rest;
And if you do fill us a bowl of your small,
may the devil take butler, bowl and all.

Come all pretty maidens, I hope there is one,
Don't let these wassailers stand out in the cold.
Step up to the door and pull back the pin,
And let those jolly wassailers in.

With variations, similar rituals continued for perhaps a century. Explanations for the thirteen fires included that they represented Jesus Christ and the apostles. The thirteenth, taken to symbolise Judas Iscariot, was quickly doused, and the materials scattered. At Phocle Farm, near Upton Bishop, though, the thirteen were either the Virgin Mary and the twelve apostles or the Old Woman and her twelve children. A variation at Ross was twelve fires in a horseshoe pattern, with a pole in the centre crowned with a human effigy known as the Maiden or the Mary. This, too, was burned. According to two commentators, R. Hogg and H.G. Bull, some form of the ritual was observed 'at many of the principal farms in the neighbourhood of Ross' until 1876, 'but in that year the ill-feeling produced by the Labourers' Union put an end to much of the festivities, and though the ill-feeling is now happily passing away, the thirteen fires are scarcely likely to become general again'.

At Ledbury the thirteenth fire was affectionately known as Old Meg, though others called it the witch. The Ledburians gathered around it to drink warm cider, eat plum cake, and toast their master and his crops.

At Eardisland more drinking went on in the oxen's—later the cows'—stalls, with toasts such as:

Here's to the plough, the fleece and the pail.
May the landlord ever flourish and the tenant never fail.

And:

Here's to thee champion, to thy white horn,
Here's God send the master a good crop of corn,
Of wheat, rye, barley and all sorts of grain;
If we live to this time twelvemonth we'll drink his health again.

Specific animals might be addressed:

> Here's to the heifer [by its name] and to the white teat,
> Wishing the mistress a house full of meat,
> With cruds [curds], milk and butter fresh every day,
> And God grant the young men keep out of her way.

At Ledbury the song concluded:

> The leaves they are green and the nuts they are brown,
> They all hang so high they cannot come down.
> They cannot come down until the next year,
> So thee eat thy oats and we'll drink our beer [or cider].

At Tretire the oxen were excused work throughout the twelve days of Christmas in commemoration of Christ's birth in an ox's stall. There, if the holed cake were thrown forward it belonged to the bailiff; back, and it went to the boys. Elsewhere the forward fall favoured the cowman; the backward, the dairymaid. Some places thought the former denoted good luck; the latter, bad. Thomas Hardy's poem, *The Oxen*, begins:

> Christmas Eve, and twelve of the clock.
> 'Now they are all on their knees',
> An elder said as we sat in a flock
> By the embers in hearthside ease.
>
> We pictured the meek mild creatures where
> They dwelt in their strawy pen,
> Nor did it occur to one of us there
> To doubt they were kneeling then.

The notion that oxen knelt lingered in Herefordshire until the early twentieth century, but on Twelfth Night rather than on Christmas Eve. Mrs. Leather remarked that she had 'talked to many people who believed this'. She did not see Kilvert's diary—it was not published till after her death—but it has an entry (5 January 1878) which reports the experience at Staunton-on-Wye of 'old James Meredith'. 'I was watching then on old Christmas Eve and at 12 o'clock the oxen that were standing knelt down upon their knees and those that were lying rose up on their knees and there they stayed kneeling and moaning, the tears running down their faces'. A different account, published in 1924, relates how at Michaelchurch a man had witnessed 'the oxen falling on their knees, sighing and groaning piteously, with tears rolling from their eyes in torrents'.

*Holy Thorn at King's Thorn (Marjorie Wight)*

Another renowned phenomenon, still on Twelfth Night, was the flowering of the holy thorn—a variety of the common hawthorn (*Crataegus monogyna*, *'Biflora'*) which flowers both in winter and summer. The original thorn at Glastonbury in Somerset claims descent from the staff of Joseph of Arimathea, which rooted in the ground as he leaned on it. Cuttings from the Glastonbury tree or its scions were widely distributed to different parts of the country.

With his usual interest in such matters Kilvert went in January 1878 to Dolfach to see the holy thorn blooming there. He was given a sprig from it. A year later he noted 'Last night the slip of Holy Thorn which John Parry of Dolfach grafted for me last spring in the vicarage lower garden blossomed in an intense frost'. Mrs. Leather remarked in 1912 that the Bredwardine tree was dead, but listed others surviving at Colwall, Dorstone, King's Thorn, Rowlstone, Stoke Edith, Tyberton and Wormsley. One could add to these further specimens at Acton Beauchamp (Redmarley Farm), Eardisland, Eaton Bishop, Fromes Hill, Llangarron (Old Gore) and Orcop (Little Hill).

Nearly all of these are now gone. The tree at Acton Beauchamp was cut down because of the nuisance occasioned by the large numbers of people who went to see it. The farmer soon afterwards broke an arm and a leg, and his house burnt down. At Eardisland the tree—in the orchard of a house called the Brouch—died in 1946, struck by lightning. Near Colliers Bridge (on ground called the 'Mounts') at Fromes Hill people went to see the phenomenon until at least the 1950s, when the tree blew down, and many still remember it. At Orcop the thorn grew beside a ruined forge close to the Maltsters Inn (now The Stars) at Little Hill. In the late 1940s it attracted cars and coaches full of people on Twelfth Night, but interest gradually waned, and the number of visitors fell to a handful. In January 1980 the tree blew down in a gale.

It was once the custom to send the monarch a cutting each year from the Glastonbury thorn. One year Charles I was staying near Much Birch when his cutting arrived. He ordered it to be planted close by, and the place came to be called King's Thorn. Others were propagated from it, and there is one descendant by a narrow lane at Little Birch. In a revival of the earlier custom, sprigs from a holy thorn in the churchyard of St. John's, Glastonbury, were sent every Christmas to the queen and her mother.

Another of the profusion of Twelfth Night customs was that of wassailing cider apple trees. Although there seems to be no early record of this from Herefordshire, one account from Worcestershire places the celebration in the 1870s on the banks of the Teme:

> Twelve small fires were lighted on an elevated wheat field and a large fire in the centre of the small ones; this large fire was sometimes 'Old Meg'. The wassailing party, forming a circle round the large fire, drank

*Apple tree wassailing at Much Marcle, 1987 (John Howes)*

201

healths, with much hurrahing, and then went to the orchard. Standing round one of the best-bearing trees, they sprinkled the tree with cider, one of the party singing the lines:

> Here's to thee, old apple tree,
> Whence thou may'st bud,
> And whence thou may'st blow,
> And whence thou may'st
> Bear apples enow.
> Hats full and caps full,
> Bushels full and sacks full,
> And my pockets full too.

Then the party returned to the farmhouse where a bountiful supper and a large quantity of cider was served.

Over a century later the custom was not so much revived in Herefordshire as introduced, and merged with elements drawn from records of indigenous wassailing. It seems that the credit for this belongs to members of Leominster Morris, who wassailed Thompson's Orchard at Yarpole in January 1984. In subsequent years they visited further orchards, some private, and some belonging to cider firms such as Dunkertons, Symonds and Westons.

The revival seems to have taken firm root. In January 2002 not only were Leominster Morris wassailing at Pembridge (starting from and returning to the New Inn), but other ceremonies took place at Marlbrook, near Leominster (at an orchard owned by Bulmers), at Much Marcle (a private occasion), and possibly elsewhere in the county. Despite its hybrid origins, the occasion, with its music, song, lanterns, fires blazing in the dark of winter, exerts a powerful pull. If only as a colourful happening, it has a worthy place in the calendar.

## February

The first of Leominster's six annual fairs was held on 13 February, the second on the first Tuesday after Mid-Lent Sunday (see below). Both were for the sale of cattle, sheep, pigs, horses, hops and 'pedlary ware'.

Ninety years ago Mrs. Leather described the custom of sending valentines as 'dying, not yet extinct'. She would have been surprised at the profusion of greetings now sent, and scandalised at such things as strippagrams. Country people used to believe that even the birds chose their mates on St. Valentine's Day (14 February).

Depending on the date of Easter, Lent begins on a Wednesday between 3 February and 9 March. The previous day is Shrove Tuesday, which used to be the occasion for horseplay, mischief-making and cruel sports such as cock-fighting. More sedate was the custom at Cradley of the children's assembling at noon and joining hands to encircle the church.

The custom of making pancakes on Shrove Tuesday now seems to be waning—but one makes such comments at one's peril. Mrs. Leather observed that Mothering Sunday was 'by no means forgotten, but declining'. Now it is flourishing as never before. In earlier times this was the occasion in Mid-Lent (the fourth Sunday) when grown children, particularly girls, were expected to visit their mothers. Taking a simnel cake as a present, and being given a celebratory meal in return, preferably of veal.

In 1589 three Bosbury men, Richard Kent, John Watkins and James Leeth, fell foul of the Church for 'going a hodiwinking on Shrove Sunday tempore vespertinarum pre[cor]um'; that is, for capering about in some form of carnival disguise at the time of the evening service. One wonders when Bosbury next had a happening of similar liveliness.

## March

Easter Day is a moveable feast depending on the moon and falling between 22 March and 25 April. Good Friday was thought to be a particularly auspicious day for planting, especially for the seeds of stocks; if these were set as the sun went down their flowers would be double. Bread or hot-cross buns baked on Good Friday might be saved and hung up for good luck. After being kept until the following Easter they could be grated into a liquid which was then drunk to ease stomach-ache. Hot-cross buns were once baked only on a Good Friday but now they are on sale in some bakers' shops and supermarkets for several weeks.

Bakers themselves kept some buns, reminding people that as Christ was on his way to be crucified a washerwoman threw some dirty water over him whereas a woman carrying newly baked bread wiped him dry and gave him a loaf. Christ then said 'From henceforth blessed be the baker and cursed be the washer'. It follows that washing clothes should be avoided on Good Friday. It was even considered unlucky to leave suds in a tub or boiler over Good Friday.

The rolling of decorated hard-boiled eggs by children at Churchill Gardens in Hereford was instituted on Good Friday in 1975 and has continued each year ever since. This is an example of a custom consciously transplanted from elsewhere but taking root locally.

Some Herefordshire villages shared with the Forest of Dean and Wales the custom of decking graves with flowers on Easter Sunday—or in some cases Palm Sunday, which was known as Flowering Sunday. Kilvert remarks on this in connection with Radnorshire.

A favoured Easter diversion was heaving, pronounced 'aving or 'oving, depending on one's area. Originally this had a religious significance to do with Christ's rising from the dead, but it became a secular celebration. In Herefordshire women were hoved on Easter Monday by other women. A party would go round farms and houses, the youngest girl carrying a bunch of flowers. They went in and sang 'Jesus Christ is risen again', then each woman in the household was in turn put in a chair and lifted. Her feet were sprinkled with drops of water from the girl's flowers, which were dipped in a basin beforehand. On Easter Tuesday the men conducted a similar exercise.

In Herefordshire 'it degenerated into wickedness, and is now discontinued', according to a comment of 1887. Detailed documentation is unfortunately not provided. A century later heaving was revived, and featured at the Ledbury Folk Fair in 1989. This was the week before Easter. Women and men took turns to lift each

*Heaving—as it was in the eighteenth century*

other on the same day. Kissing was restored to the ceremony, and the spectators contributed to a collection for charity. In the next two years the decorated chairs had increased to three, but the revival may have been short-lived.

## April

All Fools' Day (1 April) continues to have an appeal, though it is far from being a major festival. Orleton Fair was held on 23 April (St. George's Day), the traditional date when the cuckoo was expected to be first heard. At Monnington on May Eve (30 April) people renewed the birch and rowan twigs nailed outside barns and houses to keep witches at bay. Rogationtide—Rogation Sunday, the fifth after Easter, can fall in April or May—was the classic time for beating parish bounds (see chapter 3). The Leominster Morrismen mark the poet, Wordsworth's, connection with Herefordshire by dancing on his birthday each year at the commemorative stone near Leysters. They also dance near Leominster on May Day (see chapter 9).

*Heaving—as it was in the late twentieth century*

## May

May Day was once one of the highlights of the year. After the Restoration some of its customs gravitated to 29 May but many remained. In Herefordshire the expression 'maffering' meant 'gone to May Fair' and, by extension, having a good time. Hereford May Fair is still held though now purely for pleasure rather than the sale of goods which was the case in much earlier times. The earliest extant charter—and fairs were permitted only by charter from the king or some great noble—dates from the early twelfth century, though this may have confirmed an even earlier grant, for the event was also known as St. Ethelbert's Fair. The rights were vested in the bishop, which gave the alternative name of Bishop's Fair. Tolls could be levied on goods. Those offending during the nine days of the fair could be brought to summary trial before a Court of Piepowder, whose name derives from the French, *pieds poudrés* (dusty feet), which was an apt designation for the fair-goers. Successive bishops of Hereford (or rather their bailiffs) ran the fair for many centuries, starting every year on 19 May, until the rights passed to Hereford Corporation in 1838. Even then the bishop received an annual payment of 12½ bushels of the best wheat in compensation. In 1951 a full civic proclamation of the fair took place, in commemoration of the Festival of Britain which was held that year.

At Hereford May Day was also the occasion for madrigal singing from the top of the cathedral tower. The custom lapsed for almost a century before being revived in 1988. Still in Hereford, sweeps and milkmaids celebrated on 1 May. Writing in 1879, 'Nonagenarian', recalled:

*Jack in the Green (1830), after the painting by J.M. Ince,
one of the May Day events*

We used to go every May-day to Broomy-hill, and dance round the
May-pole, and play at stool-ball, and have cake and cider; and the milk-
women used to dance with the milk-pails on their heads. They used to
dress the pails with all sorts of beautiful silver things, which they
borrowed, and they used to shine in the sun, and as the women danced
so these spoons and cream jugs, and all these things, used to make
music along with the fiddle.

*Singers on top of Hereford Cathedral tower
celebrate Queen Victoria's Jubilee in 1897*

On the same day on Sweeps' Green at Broomy Hill the chimney sweeps 'took their brooms and made merry'.

The classic May ritual involving 'joy and gratitude to providence on the return of spring' was described by John Duncumb in 1804:

> On the first day of May, the juvenile part of both sexes rise early in the morning, and, walking to some neighbouring wood, supply themselves with green branches of trees. Returning home, the boughs are placed against the doors and houses, and are kept there during the remainder of the day.

In addition, maypoles—often birch trees—were brought back. One was photographed at Upper Chilstone (Madley) in 1924.

Writing just four years after Duncumb, Jonathan Williams provided this enthusiastic account:

*Maypole at Upper Chilstone, Madley (Alfred Watkins)*

Early upon the first morning of the genial month of May, young persons of both sexes repair to Eaton-hill, a small but very pleasing eminence within half a mile of the town [of Leominster] situate on the banks of the meandering Lugg and skirted with wood, where, in Leland's time, they sported and played, but where, as more conformably to the present practice, they hail the new-born spring, and extol the powers of that soul-enchanting season, in renovating the teeming earth, in cloathing the fields with green shooting herbage and variegated flowers, in sprinkling the hedges with the verdant bud, in arraying the trees with their soft livery, in perfuming the air with the fragrant odours of the apple blossom, and, in short, gladdening the whole face of reanimated nature.

In 1845, rather more prosaically, Richard Parry of Kington recorded: 'The custom of cutting the branches of trees, particularly the birch, to decorate the doors is still continued in this town and vicinity'.

Some towns held their hiring or mop fairs early in May: Bromyard on the first, and Leominster on the second, for example (see also chapter 7). Straightforward fairs included Pembridge's, on 12 May. The full list of fairs held in Herefordshire was once surprisingly long. F. & A. Merrick, printers of High Street, Hereford, issued this in 1831:

Brampton Bryan, June 22.

Bromyard, last Monday in January, Thursday before March 25, May 3, Whit Monday, Thursday before July 25, Thursday before October 29.

Dorstone, April 27, May 18, September 27, November 18.

Hereford, Tuesday after February 2, Easter Wednesday, May 19, July 1, October 20, Great Market - Wednesday after St Andrew's Day.

Huntington, July 18, November 13.

Kingsland, October 10.

Kington, Wednesday before February 2, Wednesday before Easter, Whit Monday, August 2, September 19, October 26.

Ledbury, Monday after February 1, Monday before Easter, May 12, June 22, first Tuesday in August, October 2, Monday before December 21.

Leintwardine, May 15, November 6.

*Hereford May Fair*

Leominster, February 18, Tuesday after Mid-Lent Sunday, May 2,
     July 10, September 4, November 8, third Friday in December.
Longtown, April 29, September 21.
Orleton, April 24.
Pembridge, May 12, November 22.
Ross, Holy Thursday (Corpus Christi, the Thursday after Trinity
     Sunday), July 20, Thursday after October 10, December 11,
     Great Market - Thursday after March 10.
Weobley, Holy Thursday
Wigmore, May 6, August 5.

After the battle of Worcester in 1651 the future Charles II eluded pursuing parliamentary soldiers by hiding in an oak tree at Boscobel House in Shropshire; birds—one version says an owl—perching in the tree remained undisturbed, and flew off only at the approach of the troopers who concluded that no one could be hiding there. When Charles was formally restored to the throne on 29 May (in 1660) this date, combined with commemorative oak leaves and sprays, came to be regarded in many places as the real May Day.

Until well within living memory children sported sprigs of oak on Oak Apple Day (the same 29 May), in default of which their fellows would sting their bare arms or legs with nettles. One village is reputed to keep up the custom still: Dilwyn. As late as the 1930s at Bromyard 'you'd see Maypoles all the way down Sheep Street, decorated with oak boughs and flowers, and people dancing round them, all wearing oak leaves'. Every house in Bosbury had its spray of oak over the door, and at Kingsland a great bough was hoisted to the top of the church tower.

The Heart of Oak Friendly Society at the village of Fownhope has its club gathering

*Fownhope procession, ?1950s (Marjorie Wight)*

on the nearest Saturday to Oak Apple Day. Sticks bearing wooden oak apples and fresh flowers are paraded to the church for a service, preceded by the club's banner and oak bough with red, white and blue ribbons.

Before the institution of national health insurance, early in the twentieth century, benefit clubs to which members contributed a few pence weekly were widespread. There were two in Eardisland alone: the Foresters and the Druids. In the 1880s the Druids had 110 members who marched in procession on Whit Monday (Whitsunday, seven weeks after Easter, falls between 14 May and 10 June), headed by band, banner and club officials, to a service at the church, then round local farms. A meal in the parish room followed, and then came toasts and songs.

## June

King's Caple's club feast, which included dancing on the tump near the church and nine-pin bowling, was held on Whit Tuesday. June was a great month for fairs (see above) and also village wakes—originally solemn celebrations of church foundations but latterly characterised, at least according to some observers, by swearing, drinking, quarrelling and fighting. 'The alehouses are filled with noisy visitors, and resounding with oaths and songs, and roaring laughter', wrote the anonymous author of *A Serious Address on the Subject of Wakes, or Feasts*, published in 1820 (and printed, incidentally, by T.B. Watkins at the Albion Press, High Town, Hereford, for whom see chapter 8). Writing some 60 years later, the Webbs offer a similar view:

> A merry-making was ever a favourite opportunity for settling old grudges, and usually ended in a broil. So among the boors of Wormelow, Huntington, and other hundreds, wounds and deaths have been till of late years too frequently the accompaniment of these annual feasts, that were originally instituted for the cultivation of religious and moral feelings, the promotion of charity and peace.

On the other hand, participants held those events in great affection. Each feast, wrote Mrs. Leather, 'had a special dainty associated with it. ... At Ross it was pork and turnips; at Peterchurch, rice pudding and currants ... Blakemere had a cherry feast; the people of the parish also had their first roast duck and green peas that day'. The delicacy at Brampton Bryan was Bron Fair Cakes, similar to Shrewsbury Cakes, on 22 June, when until 1970 a horse fair took place.

On Midsummer Eve (23 June), according to John Aubrey, 'In Herefordshire ... they make fires in the Fields in the waies: *sc.* [understand] to Blesse the Apples'. This was written late in the seventeenth century. The only other possible reference is in a letter from Elton, two hundred years later: 'Unless the orchards are christened on St. Peter's Day [29 June], the crop will not be good', but this seems to refer to a hope for rain rather than an allusion to any form of ceremony.

## July

Wakes and fairs continued in July. At Huntington (near Kington) from 1403 till 1956 a fair associated with St. Thomas à Becket was held during the month. Richard de Brito, one of Thomas's murderers, built the church and dedicated it to him in an attempt at expiation. St. Thomas's relics were translated on 7 July 1220, and the fair was held on the 18th, the difference in dates perhaps being due to the change in the calendar again. Originally all forms of livestock were sold; latterly, only horses, including the mountain ponies known as 'munts'. The animal reaching the highest price of the day was ceremonially ridden through the public house in the village. At one time the numbers of the horses meant that they occupied over a mile of road, but by the mid-twentieth century the fair had almost completely died out.

*Huntington Church*

Richard de Brito as a further penance paid for the north chapel to be built in the old church at Dorstone. His workmen are said to have been housed in the village at the Pandy Inn, which claims to be the oldest licensed premises in Herefordshire.

Withington's feast was kept on the first Sunday in July, and Lugwardine's on the second. Fred Arrowsmith said that on the latter occasion his father always dug up the first of his new potatoes. The old merrymakings are now replaced by school and village fêtes (at Huntington a fête was initiated by Dr. and Mrs. Jack) and events such as Bromyard's town gala.

## August

On Lammas Day (1 August) common land which had been fenced off while hay grew was thrown open again for pasture. The meadows by the River Lugg at Lugwardine preserve many features of the mediaeval system. Land is still in strips, with boundaries marked by 'mere stones', many of which bear their owners' initials, and some are dated. The management of the meadows is overseen by the commoners' association which carries on the function of the old manorial court. In 2000 Anthea Brian traced well over 50 former Lammas meadows, spread through the Arrow, Dore, Frome, Lugg, Teme and Wye Valleys.

## September

The fifth fair of the year at Leominster, on 4 September, was noted 'for the hiring of hop-pickers, great numbers of whom come from Wales' (see also chapter 7). Leominster's horse races were also held in September.

The Bromyard Folk Festival was founded in 1967 on the initiative of Dave Jones. From an initial budget of £125 it grew to a multi-thousand pound event, and one of the premier festivals for traditional folk music. Jones continued to organise it for 24 years until his untimely death in 1991. Each year, a gathering of some 2,000 people from all over the country is entertained by singers, musicians and morris dancers. The festival-goers are far from passive, and many—perhaps most—join in the singing, dancing and story-telling, not to speak of the drinking. Neither the fuel blockade of 2000 nor the foot and mouth crisis of 2001 caused an interruption in the festival, which continues on the second full weekend of the month.

## October

This was one of the classic months for mops (see chapter 7).

Hallowe'en (31 October) was feared rather than celebrated in the past, but parties are a fairly common occurrence now. However, they seldom include the attempts at divining a future husband which used to be made on the day by young women (see chapter 4). Some children have taken to going round in fancy dress, knocking on doors and demanding a 'trick or treat'. The practice has been condemned as an import from America but it originally travelled there from this country.

## November

Guy Fawkes' Night (5 November) is still a lively, popular festival, though some of the rhymes and chants associated with it have fallen out of use. In Herefordshire boys marched round shouting:

> Remember, remember the fifth of November,
> Gunpowder, treason and plot.
> Remember, remember the fifth of November
> Shall never be forgot.

Parry of Kington describes a very lively scene:

> The morning is ushered in by ringing a peal or two, and in the evening
> stakes are removed from fences, branches cut from trees, and secured for
> making bonfires on the upper and lower crosses. Some old persons have
> remembered when upwards of a load of wood was thus used to supply
> the bonfires, which were first made with straw, one or more were some-
> times burned upon gibbets several feet high, at a late hour of the night,
> the boys shouting forth the words of the motto, with loud huzzas, and
> running up to the persons passing along the street with saying - 'Pray
> remember Guy', while fireworks, squibs, serpents, crackers, &c., are
> flung about in every direction by the aged as well as the young; many
> riders have fallen from their horses and persons injured in the streets by
> the lawless multitude inflamed by drink, and fighting their way against
> each other.

He concludes by remarking sadly on the expense involved, saying that if the
money were given to the poor it 'could tend to make them comfortable and
happy'. Yet the poor were the most enthusiastic participants on this and similar
occasions.

### December

The boy bishop ceremony takes place at Hereford Cathedral on the nearest
Saturday to St. Nicholas's Day, 6 December (see chapter 3). St. Thomas's Day
(21 December) was another of the occasions during the winter when people
were by tradition allowed to collect money and supplies. The activity was
called thomasing, gooding or mumping. In Herefordshire a sack of wheat was
set at every farmhouse door and any woman who called to ask was given a
quartern measure of it.

At Monkland an annual dole for poorer people provided by Sir Henry
Williams Baker on St. Thomas's Day. After a service in the church at which the
hymn, *O praise our God and King* was invariably sung, bags of grain were
given out. In cold weather the poor received bowls of hot soup at Horkesley
House.

The custom had earlier been rather more elaborate, and also more lively. A
correspondent wrote from Ross to the *Gentleman's Magazine* in February 1819,
with reference to the previous December:

> At Christmas time they go a *mumping*, as it is called, mostly on St.
> Thomas's-day, and they receive from the farmers a small dish of wheat;
> from other houses a trifling donation. The feast of the Church is observed
> with great conviviality, and ale-house balls, and dinners; nor do they
> separate till the money, which they lay up for weeks before, is spent;
> cock-fighting at such seasons is a favourite amusement.

Wassailing in the form of touring houses and farms does not seem to have been widely prevalent in Herefordshire—as it was, for example, in Gloucestershire. Wassail itself means 'be well', and the bowl carried round was replenished with more or less anything alcoholic but ideally with a punch made of hot cider, gin, nutmeg and sugar. Mrs. Leather met a man who as a boy at Ullingswick, near Bromyard, went *wassilling*:

> We had a captain who kept the punch-bowl or wassill bowl. It was a great big one made o' beech wood, and would hold a large quantity, perhaps two gallons. They took it round at night, decorated with ribbons and coloured streamers, beginning some little time before Christmas, and visiting all the houses in the neighbourhood. They sang songs and carols, and one special carol beginning:
>> Wassail, wassail round the town,
>> Your bread is white, your ale is brown.

At Tretire on Christmas Eve the wassail song was back in the stable as part of the ceremony clearly deriving from practice elsewhere in the county on Twelfth Night. With a cake placed on the horns of an ox 'they say certain words, begging a good crop for the master'. If the ox throws the cake forward it belongs to the men; behind to the boys. They take with them a wooden bottle of cider, and drink it, repeating, the charm before mentioned'.

Ivy and holly were brought in as decorations only on Christmas Eve, and taken down on Candlemas Day (2 February). The Yule log was drawn to the

*The Old Wonder Morris at the Butcher's Arms, Woolhope,*
*on Boxing Day, 1991*

*Apple tree wassail by the Leominster Morris*

fireplace. People would carefully preserve fragments for the ensuing year, since among other things they warded off lightning.

On Christmas Day the morris dancers or mummers (see chapter 9) might come round, or carol singers (chapter 8). At the village of Blakemere a holy thorn bloomed at midnight (as others did on Twelfth Night). Boxing Day was once the time for killing the wren, a most unlucky bird to kill on any other day. John Masefield remembered from his youth that 'some young savages still killed the wren on St. Stephen's Day' (26 December). What is still hunted on Boxing Day is the fox. In 2001 hunts met at Ledbury and Leominster after their lay-off because of the foot and mouth epidemic, though they faced an uncertain future in the light of possible legislation.

Fred Arrowsmith of Lugwardine remembered a Boxing Day custom which seems to have been a relic of wassailing. The pub landlord would 'produce a large bowl and put into it a sample of every kind of drink in his house. Toasted pieces of bread were added, and whenever a customer bought a drink, this was put in as well. A glassful of the concoction was ladled out for the customer with an added piece of toast'.

At the inn at Lower Ballingham there was always a broom dance at the inn on Boxing morning, to the accompaniment of a fiddle normally kept behind the bar. Further dancing, cider drinking and singing followed. There were all kinds of songs, but this one was never missed out:

*Meeting of the hounds at Stretton Grandison (M. Wight)*

We wish you a merry Christmas, a happy New Year,
A pocket full of money and a cellar full of beer,
And a good fat pig to serve you all the year.

Within a few days New Year's Eve would loom, and with it bush burning and a fresh cycle of seasonal customs.

# Bibliography

Unless otherwise stated the place of publication of books listed is London.

Anderson, Joseph, *The Witch on the Wall. Medieval Erotic Sculpture in the British Isles* (Copenhagen and London, 1977)

Anderson, William, *Green Man* (1990)

Anon., Manuscript Song Book (Hereford Record Office, AD 41/1)

    *Old Meg of Herefordshire for a Mayd Marian* (London, 1609; Malvern, 1982)

    'The Civil War in Herefordshire', *The Antiquary*, 1 (1870), 120-1

Arrowsmith, Fred, *Lugwardine. Church and Village Fifty to Sixty Ago* (np, nd)

Aubrey, John, *Brief Lives*, ed. John Buchanan-Brown (2000)

Bannister, A.T., *The Place-names of Herefordshire. Their origin and Development* (Hereford, 1916)

    'Sutton Walls and the Legend of St. Ethelbert', *Woolhope Trans.* (1917), 221-6

    'William Langland's Birthplace', *Woolhope Trans.*, 5 (1924-6), 3-7

Barber, W.D., 'Notes on Tretyre Church', *Woolhope Trans.* (1908-11; issued 1914), 137-143

Barthrop, Chris, 'Wassail This About, Then?', *Folklore*, 113, no.1 (2002), 42-3

Bede, Cuthbert (Edward Bradley), 'Modern Mumming', *Notes and Queries*, 2nd ser., 40 (1861), 271-2

Bentley, Samuel, *A Short Account of the Church ... in Bosbury* (London and Derby, 1881)

    *History and Description of the Parish of Bosbury* (1891)

*Between the Wars. Linton, Upton Bishop and Aston Ingham, 1920-1940* (Linton, 1993)

Bishop, Lewis C., 'Walter Map', *Herefordshire Magazine*, 2, 414-7

Blake, William A., *Parish of Burghill, Herefordshire* (np, 1972)

Blount, Thomas, *Tenures of Land and Customs of Manors*, ed. W.C. Hazlitt (1874; orig. 1784-1815; written 1679)

Botzum, Richard and Catherine, *A History of Lucton* (np, ? 1985)

Bowater, Veronica, *The Church of Saint Mary Magdalene, Leintwardine* (Leintwardine, 1978)

Brian, Anthea, 'Lammas Meadows in Herefordshire, pp. 205-218 in *A Herefordshire Miscellany*, ed. D. Whitehead and J. Eisel (Hereford, 2000)

Bright, Allan H. 'Colwall and the Neighbourhood', *Woolhope Trans.* (1921-3, issued 1925), 178-184

    *New Light on 'Piers Plowman'* (1928)

Broadwood, Lucy, and Fuller Maitland, J.A. (eds) *English County Songs* (1893)

Brooks, Edward C., *The Life of Saint Ethelbert* (np, 1996)

Bull, H.G., 'Mistletoe in Herefordshire', *Woolhope Trans.*, 1 (1852-65, issued 1907), 312-347

Bulmer, E.F., 'The evolution of Herefordshire cyder', in *Memorials of Old Herefordshire*, ed. Compton Reade (1904)

Bushaway, Bob, *By Rite. Custom Ceremony and Community in England, 1700-1880* (1982)

Capes, Canon, *The Bishop's Fair* (Hereford, n.d.)

Card, H., *A Dissertation on the Subject of the Herefordshire Beacon* (1822)

Cave, E.L., 'The Burning of the Bush', *Woolhope Trans.* (1898), 5-8

Cawte, E.C., Helm, Alex, and Peacock, N., *English Ritual Drama* (1967)

Coleman, Delphine, *Orcop. The Story of a Herefordshire Village* (Hanley Swan, 1992)

Crawford, Phyllis, *In England Still* (Bristol, 1938)

Davies, Gwiliym, and Paimer, Roy (eds.), *Let Us Be Merry. Traditional Christmas Songs and Carols from Gloucestershire* (Lechlade, 1996)

Davies, James, 'Our Herefordshire Customs', *Woolhope Trans.* (1877), 22-30

Davies, Owen, 'Healing Charms in England and Wales, 1700-1950', *Folklore*, 107 (1996), 19-32

Dayus, Kathleen, *Her People* (1982)

Defoe, Daniel, *A Tour through the Whole Island of Great Britain* (Harmondsworth, 1971; orig. 1724-6)

Devlin, J. Dacres, *Helps to Hereford History, ... The Mordiford Dragon; and other subjects* (1848)

Donald, J.R., *The History of Wigmore* (Leominster, nd)

Duncumb, John, *Collections towards the History and Antiquities of the County of Hereford* (2 vols, Hereford, 1804)

Dunn, George, *George Dunn. The Minstrel of Quarry Bank*, ed. Roy Palmer (Dudley, 1984)

Fitzgerald, Penelope, *The Knox Brothers* (1977)

Fletcher, H.L.V. *Herefordshire* (1948)

    *The Wye Valley* (1968)

*Folklore, Myths and Legends of Great Britain* (1973)

Forrest, John, *The History of Morris Dancing, 1458-1750* (Cambridge, 1999)

Fosbroke, Thomas Dudley, *Ariconensia; or Archaeological Sketches of Ross, and Archenfield* (Ross, 1821)

    *The Wye Tour* (Ross, 3rd ed., 1826)

Friar, Stephen, *A Companion to the English Parish Church* (Stroud, 1996)

Garnett, David, *The Eardisley Diamond* (np, 1994)

Gaunt, Peter, *The Cromwellian Gazetteer* (Gloucester, 1987)

Gibbings, Robert, *Coming Down the Wye* (1942)

Golding, C., 'Herefordshire New Year Customs', *The Antiquary* 3 (Jan. 1873), 7

Grigson, Geoffrey, *The Englishman's Flora* (St. Albans, 1958)

Grindrod, Charles F., *The Shadow of the Raggedstone* (1888)

Grinsell, L.V., 'Alfred Watkins and and The Old Straight Track', *Woolhope Trans.*, 46, pt 1 (1988-90), 76-81

    'Hangman's Stones', *Folklore*, 96, pt 2 (1985), 217-222

Haggard, Andrew, *Dialect and Local Usages of Herefordshire* (1972)

Hamer, Fred (ed.), *Garners Gay* (1967)

    *Green Groves* (1973)

Handy, Thony, *No Borders. Poems from Herefordshire* (Hereford, 1985)

Havergal, F.T., *Herefordshire Words and Phrases* (Walsall, 1887)